Manna Songs:
Stories of Jewish Culture & Heritage

Edited by Diane Gottlieb

Foreword by Erika Dreifus

Copyright © 2025 Individual Contributors as Named Herein

All rights reserved. No part of this publication may be reproduced, distributed, or transmitted in any form or by any means, including photocopying, recording, or other electronic or mechanical methods, without the prior written permission of the publisher, except in the case of brief quotations embodied in critical reviews and certain other noncommercial uses permitted by copyright law. For permission requests, write to the publisher at the address below.

ELJ Editions, Ltd. is committed to publishing works of quality and integrity. In that spirit, we are proud to offer this work of creative nonfiction to our readers; however, the story, the experiences, and the words are the individual authors' alone. The events are portrayed to the best of the individual authors' memory and some names and identifying details have been changed to protect the privacy of the people involved.

ISBN: 978-1-942004-90-5

Library of Congress Control Number: 2025940277

Cover art by Aliza Marton

ELJ Editions, Ltd.
P.O. Box 815
Washingtonville, NY 10992
www.elj-editions.com

Praise for *Manna Songs*

What a powerful look at what it means to celebrate Jewish joy, to preserve the past, and to forge our Jewish identities in today's tumultuous world. Here's to uplifting Jewish stories.
 —Zibby Owens, *On Being Jewish Now: Reflections of Authors and Advocates*

The collection of essays in *Manna Songs* celebrates the rich, complex, and deeply meaningful experience of being Jewish today. Each essay presents a unique and accessible perspective on the Jewish experience. As a whole, the collection covers topics ranging from food, history, literature, religious practice, joy, sorrow, and legacy. This beautiful collection showcases an abundance of voices all raised in a common song. Do not miss this gorgeous chorus!
 —Christie Tate, author of NYT bestseller *GROUP: How One Therapist and a Circle of Strangers Saved My Life* and *B.F.F.: A Memoir of Friendship Lost & Found*

These are wonderful stories—short, touching vignettes of Jewish life, resilience, humor and pride. A book that is needed in our trying times.
 —Rabbi David Wolpe, author of *David: The Divided Heart*

To read the deeply personal essays in *Manna Songs* is to get a kaleidoscopic view of Judaism bursting with so much color, flavor, fragrance and music, it's a veritable buffet for all five senses. Rich in symbolism and emotion, this collection is full of descriptions of trinkets and mementos- a bracelet, a toy solider, a Viking hammer and even a plastic fork- which serve as a core around which each author builds their narrative about their own Jewish lineage. *Manna Songs* is a reminder of how, in an ever changing world, Judaism-Jewishness- is constant, eternal and steadfast no matter how far back into the past or forward into the future we peer.
 —Gila Pfeffer, author of *Nearly Departed: Adventures in Loss, Cancer and Other Inconveniences*

Fierce, funny, illuminating, and tender, *Manna Songs* is a remarkable collection of essays. Informed by the ancient religious and cultural traditions of a people who, as contributor Lisa Grunberger puts it, "...contain Jewish multitudes," in these pages writers of all ages and walks of life illumine modern-day Jewish life. The painful history of their ancestry is real and never glossed over, but as real is the writers' ever-present joy and celebration of love and light. In the words of contributor Matthew Lippman: "To be a Jew, I have come to realize, is the great experience of the sorrow in the joy and the joy in the sorrow."

—Alison McGhee, bestselling and critically acclaimed author of books for all ages, including, most recently, *Weird Sad and Silent*.

From obsessively documenting lost synagogues to drinking Elite instant coffee for the memories to teaching in an Orthodox day school as a secular Jew, this lively collection features a wide range of perspectives on what it means to be a Jewish writer right now. The essays explore identity, history, joy, and sorrow, and making a place in this fraught world through words. This book is for those looking for a diversity of takes on the inner lives of Jewish artists, broadly defined.

—Aviya Kushner, author of *The Grammar of God* and *Wolf Lamb Bomb*

Manna Songs reminds readers that there is much more to Judaism than Holocaust remembrance, October 7, and reaction to antisemitism. These are present, but among many aspects of Jewish life, culture, and history explored in this collection. This book opens a window into Jewish life in all its richness—ritual and language, food and memory, joy and sorrow. Readers will walk away with a deeper understanding not only of Judaism, but of the inner celebrations that shape Jewish identity and life.

—Howard Lovy, author of *Found and Lost: The Jake and Cait Story*

Manna Songs is a triumphant collection of stories that celebrate and uplift the Jewish experience, honoring the culture and heritage that have defined our people for thousands of years. The essays are beautifully written and heartfelt, and sure to warm your soul like your bubbe's matzah ball soup on a Friday night.

—Heidi Shertok, author of *Unorthodox Love*

Manna Songs is full of memoir stories of Jewish joy, a joy often presented through travel, especially resulting from the mid twentieth century when Jewish flux was widespread. And they are full of food. Food that reminds us what it is to be Jewish. Like the manna described in *The Book of Exodus* (16:1-36.) Then too the Jews were on the move, wandering in the desert, and fed by a Godly food that fell from the sky. According to the commentaries the manna fell twice a day like snow and when you put it in your mouth it tasted like your favorite food. These stories that stretch from a Passover seder in the Himalayas to the sanctity of a Bubbe's kitchen in New York are full of what we inherit as Jews: community, love and warmth. That is Jewish joy!

–Rachel Neve-Midbar, author of *Salaam of Birds*.

What a stunning collection. These essays offer a richly personal immersion in Jewishness as we bear witness to the reading of the Haggadah and the Seder meal at table after table, each one the same, yet beautifully singular. We dissolve into the rhythms of Rosh Hashanah, wander the hallways of Jewish day school, hover in the silvery stillness of Shabbat, and feel the ever-present weight and shadow of the Holocaust. But this kaleidoscopic exploration—this celebration of what it means to be Jewish—is also an ode, an homage, and a love song to the complicated and gorgeous texture of thirty-two distinct lives and the beloved people within them: a comic grandmother who bonds through dirty jokes but can't quite reach her daughter; a brokenhearted college student who boards a train home for Passover because she needs her family more than ever; a 103-year-old WWII veteran who slips his granddaughter cash for a flight to Israel; a mother who loses custody of her daughter and reconciles this unbearable loss through her understanding of Torah and God. And these moments are just the beginning. Again, what a stunning collection.

–Jeannine Ouellette, author of the bestselling Substack *Writing in the Dark*

If the essays in *Manna Songs* were merely composed of vivid, rich and lyrical prose, but did not represent a range of beautifully diverse Jewish viewpoints, Dayenu.

If they represented a range of beautifully diverse Jewish viewpoints, but did not deepen my connection to Judaism, Dayenu.

If they deepened my connection to Judaism but did not introduce me to new and exciting Jewish writers, Dayenu.

If they introduced me to new and exciting Jewish writers but did not show me facets of my own tradition that weren't yet familiar to me, Dayenu.

If they showed me facets of my own tradition that weren't yet familiar to me, but didn't provide a potent infusion of Jewish joy, Dayenu.

But *Manna Songs* does all this and much more. I'm so grateful for this treasure trove of luminous and soul-sustaining Jewish perspectives.

–Elissa Wald, Editor in Chief of *JUDITH Magazine*

Table of Contents

Erika Dreifus *Foreword* i
Diane Gottlieb *Introduction* v

THE JOY OF JEWISH IDENTITY
HINENI—HERE I AM

Matthew Lippman *Hineni* 3
Aliza Marton *My Art, My Song, My Prayer* 7
Lynne Golodner *Identity in My Daily Cup* 11
Adrienne Dern *Pass the Peas* 15
Sarah Leibov *Living Without Doubt* 18
Nina B. Lichtenstein *When a Norwegian Converts to Judaism: The Viking Bar Mitzvah and Other Adventures in Jewish Joy* 22
Julia Grunes *On Jewish Life in Spain* 26
Eileen Vorbach Collins *How Shall I Hang My Mezuzah?* 30
Robbi Nester *I Am a Jewish Poet* 34
Lisa Grunberger *Turn It and Turn It Again* 37

WHAT WE CARRY: RITUALS, JUDAICA
PASSING IT ALL DOWN

Dina Elenbogen *What We Carry* 45
Sandell Morse *Papa's Tallit* 49
Joan Leegant *Inheritance* 53
Julie Zuckerman *A Sage Gift* 57
Mimi Zieman *When the Moon Calls Us* 59
Amy Rogers *Christmas Dinner Miami Style: A Hanukkah Fish Tale* 63
Talya Jankovits *Hachnasat Orchim* 67

HONORING THOSE WHO CAME BEFORE
Seth Schindler *Paradise* 75

Melinda Gordon Blum *This Isn't About a Bracelet* 80

Melissa Greenwood *A Toy Soldier Named "Papa"* 84

Ana Miriam Lublin *Jewish Joy Stuffed in My Suitcase* 88

Debbie Feit *The Power of the Plastic Fork* 92

Amy Shimshon-Santo *My Father's Floating Burial* 95

Rochelle Newman-Carrasco *Tell Me Another One* 100

CONNECTING: TO GOD
TO SYNAGOGUE
TO PRAYER
TO THE TREE OF LIFE

Judy Bolton-Fasman *Kaddish* 109

Tzivia Gover *My Akedah* 112

Jena Schwartz *My Father's Blessings, My Mother's Stones: My First D'var Torah* 117

Ellen Levitt *The Old Shul* 122

Ronit Plank *That Temple Feeling* 125

Gabrielle Ariella Kaplan-Mayer *Light in the Empty Sanctuary* 130

Megan Vered *Kaddish Confessions* 134

Jennifer Fliss *The Understory* 137

Contributors 149

Editors 149

Foreword

Erika Dreifus

> *Like manna in the desert, Jewish stories have nourished the Jewish people and long sustained them through the most challenging of times.*

This line, which appeared within the call for submissions that eventually yielded this volume, helps frame the book that you are about to read. In its seeming simplicity, the sentence anticipates not only the pride, joy, strength, and resilience that characterize the essays compiled here; it also offers a promise of the reader's experience to come.

Which is to say: If you are Jewish, spending time with these deeply personal stories will nourish and sustain you, even as you may sense yourself to be struggling day-to-day in what so many of us have indeed been finding to be another extended episode in the Jewish people's long history of "the most challenging of times." And if you happen to be a reader who doesn't identify as Jewish—let me pause here to say "thank you," truly, for being interested enough in this book to pick it up—please know that these pages welcome you, too. Warmly.

The first essayist you'll meet in *Manna Songs*, Matthew Lippman, titles his contribution "Hineni" (Hebrew for "Here I Am," or "I Am Here"), and with this statement—again, an ostensibly simple one—we grasp an essential theme that connects the essays and voices that follow, one that begins to echo for us as readers, too. ***Here we are***, not merely present and accounted for, but on a deeper and intensely significant level, fully immersed and engaged in a multifocal, multivocal examination of what it means to be Jewish.

Geographically, the varieties of "here" encompassed in this book will situate you within in an array of settings: in New York and San Francisco and Seattle (to name just a few within the United States) as well as in Israel, Scandinavia, and Spain. They travel through time, reflecting the lasting legacies of ancient rituals, texts, and teachings; the continuing influence of multi-generational family histories; and present perspectives shaped by the contributors' own diverse lived experiences and encounters in the 20th and 21st centuries.

Speaking of the present: It's important to note that although it's by no means the focus of even a single essay here—an intentional editorial choice—*Manna Songs* by necessity acknowledges the inescapable present of Jewish life after October 7, 2023. Even here, however, the focus is, in the end, a sustaining one: As contributor Sarah Leibov notes late in her essay, when she mentions her attendance at a post-October 7 Hanukkah vigil commemorating the victims and praying for the safe return of those held hostage: "I felt then that our faith is about finding light in the darkness and holding out for hope— this is how we have survived as a people."

I have not reached out to Leibov or to any of the other gifted writers whose essays in Manna Songs contain comparable gems. But speaking from my own experience, I can tell you that it's not always easy for a writer to articulate such keen and moving insights. A single sentence may have taken its author hours (or days, or longer) of composition and revision to land on the page as the reader encounters it.

Moreover, when the overall subject is Jewish identity, a Jewish writer may, paradoxically, find the assignment surprisingly exacting. Contributor Lisa Grunberger is surely not alone when she confesses, as she does at the outset of her essay: "Asking me about my Jewishness, reminds of that joke where an elder fish asks two younger fish, 'How's the water today, boys?' The younger fish says to the other: 'What the hell is water?!' Being Jewish is so much a part of who I am, I can't define or separate it out.'" And yet, each essayist here responds to that challenge of definition with artistry, honesty, and heart, yielding a collection brimming with distinct, and distinctive, responses.

Earlier, I referenced Matthew Lippman's opening essay. I'd like to conclude by citing the concluding lines from Jennifer Fliss's "The Understory," which closes the volume: "Collective nouns always fascinate me," Fliss remarks as her essay nears its end. "How a single thing is just the thing, but when there are several, they become something else, something larger, stronger." She continues: "A group of fighter jets is called a squadron. A group of trees is called a forest. A group of Jews is called a miracle."

I read those last lines in *Manna Songs*, and I paused. Almost instantly, as I began to reflect on the book I'd just finished reading—initially conceived and ultimately produced by a non-Jewish publisher at yet another moment when the Jewish people are facing "the most challenging of times"—I understood that this group of essays, too, is a miracle. Like that manna in the desert, it has nourished and sustained me. May it do the same for you.

Erika Dreifus
Author of *Quiet Americans: Stories* and *Birthright: Poems*
June 1, 2025

Introduction

Diane Gottlieb

I love to sing. Always have. I spent countless hours in my early teens, standing in front of the mirror, my hairbrush as mic, belting out everything from the Rolling Stones to Broadway show tunes. Ah, the bliss. And while I still love singing solo—I've been known to take to the karaoke stage, on occasion—there's something magical about adding one's voice to a chorus.

It was in Glen Spey, New York, at my summer sleepaway camp, that I first experienced the joy of being in song with others. Camp Ramah was a Jewish camp. We prayed there. Every morning, gathering in the small, cleared space butting against the woods, our voices lifted together, reaching the very tops of the tallest trees. As we sang Birkat Hamazon, the Jewish Grace After Meals, I could swear the cafeteria shook in response to our impassioned expression of thanks. Some of us felt God in those moments. Others, not. But, either way, the connection to our cherished ancestors, who had sung the same words, the same tunes for millennia, was palpable. That was Holy. That was Jewish joy.

Today, I think of stories as songs, with their own rhythms and melodies that nourish the soul. Who doesn't remember their favorite stories, the books we turned to when we hungered to discover who we were? Who doesn't recall the words that told us, when our hearts were broken, that we would be okay, that the world could hold us—and would. My own heart swells with appreciation and pride when I think of the breadth and depth of Jewish stories—the old tales of Rebbe Nachman and Sholem Aleichem, the Yiddish poets, the ever-growing Holocaust cannon, the current voices in fiction, nonfiction, and poetry that sing of our rich, often challenging, history, and, at the same time, of our resilience—and resistance. Of course, there's our comedy—perhaps our greatest resistance of all.

So, when Ariana D. Den Bleyker shared with me her vision of an anthology comprised of short non-fiction essays celebrating Jewish joy, and that she would like to call it *Manna Songs: Stories of Jewish Culture & Heritage*, I wanted in—all in. I have not looked back since.

What an absolute privilege and honor it has been to edit this gorgeous collection of Jewish voices. And how much I have learned about our wildly diverse and glorious tribe! We've got stories! Weddings, B'nai Mitzvot. Candlesticks, tallit, old dishes, new traditions. There are bracelets and forks, invitations and commemorations. The Catskills, Florida, the Pacific Northwest, Chicago. Mt. Everest, Israel, Denmark, Spain. We've got Jewish Vikings, Jewish poets, grandmas, grandpas, moms, dads, lovers, kids. Coffee, bookmarks, floating burials, and dreams. Synagogues, prayer, Torah—and trees. The anthology is bookended by two powerful stories about trees. Oh, to celebrate our roots, our strength, our ability to bend—and grow—in the harshest of storms.

Not all the stories in the anthology are happy ones. Several recount the harshest of storms. The joy in those stories lies in the courage of survival and in the bonds to our culture that sustain us throughout time.

Thirty-two contributors sharing their own takes on Jewish joy! How was I to organize such a magnificent bounty of stories reflecting the diversity of Jewish lives? Just as I do when seeking answers to life's most difficult questions, I turned to our tradition: I would look at these essays as commentary on specific themes—a Jewish joy version of midrash.

Manna Songs' first section is called "The Joy of Jewish Identity: Hineni—Here I Am." The essays I've included in "Hineni" trace the authors' varied journeys of discovery of their singular Jewish selves. "What We Carry: Ritual, Judaica: Passing It All Down" references ritual objects, holiday observances, and traditions that have been passed to the authors from previous generations or from important figures in their current lives. It also speaks to the meanings we choose to carry and how we choose to do so. "Honoring Those Who Came Before" features moving tributes to loved ones who have passed—and a deep appreciation for the gifts they've left behind. The final section, "Connecting to God, to Synagogue, to Prayer, to the Tree of Life," is perhaps the most spiritual of the sections. While Judaism is a culture, it is also a religion; the two are inextricably intertwined. Even Jews who are not observant or do not believe in a Divine presence, often feel deeply connected to one prayer—or several—to a portion of the Torah, to a synagogue, to *some*thing spiritually Jewish. I ended *Manna Songs* with this section because the essays within it seem to me to leave the reader with the greatest number of questions. It's a fitting ending to a book celebrating Jewish heritage, as what could be more Jewish than an unanswered question?

Jewish joy. It is indeed complex, rich, and beautiful. Its heart beats strong and fierce even through the sharpest of pains, the deepest of sorrows, the most troubling of times in history. Today, Jews are facing a shocking rise in global antisemitism. I see *Manna Songs* as a hopeful and necessary light in that darkness. I am incredibly grateful to have had the opportunity to bring such bright Jewish voices together in this powerful, uplifting chorus. May their words sustain you, reader. May their joy inspire your own song.

Diane Gottlieb
June 10, 2025

The Joy of Jewish Identity
Hineni—Here I Am

Hineni

Matthew Lippman

When I was in Rosh Hashana services everything got real quiet, real quick. I sat in the sanctuary, left of the bimah, and in front of me, floor to ceiling windows provided a view into the woods behind the holy house, giving me a front row seat, not only to the rabbi, but to the exploding autumn leaves. Yellow and orange and red and green and brown. The ecstatic death of autumn. It's a magical thing, and I found myself in a Marc Chagall dream. I found myself in a fantasy of taking off all my clothes, moving through the window, osmotically, and disappearing into the trees. Being enveloped by the trees. A communion. A union because God is not that elusive. Because God is *in* everything and because God is *of* everything. Because God is here, present, in any type of prayer that is called prayer. *Hineni*. A sweetness in the expansion of self so the self no longer exists. This Rosh Hashanah, the idea of disappearing into the world, gave me great joy and I wept because I was present.

This is the joy of being a Jew, for me. Presence and in the mode of paying attention. The absolute ability to feel sorrow and joy all at once in the silent contemplation of being. *Hineni*. Don't mess with being. Double *Hineni*.

The self and not the self. That is all I wanted. To get swallowed up by the trees while the rabbi opened the arc, *Sh'ma Yisra'eil Adonai Eloheinu Adonai echad*. And, sitting there, all that happened was that I wept. I did not know why I wept but it was everywhere and everything. During Aleinu. During the Amidah. When the shofar was ignited. Everywhere in the service the ecstatic joy came to me in an experience of tears.

Is there a language enough to speak of such a thing? A phrase? If there is, I don't know what it is, but I believe this is why I dedicated my life to writing poems. It's the mystery of the inexplicable, of trying to discover it through words and never succeeding.

Being a Jew is the sorrow and the joy, all at once, together, dancing. It's these two feelings, embedded in one body, mind, spirit. It's a constant fascination for me. It's the mystery in the unsayable that gives me the excitement and exuberant beauty of being a Jew.

When I was a kid my grandmother, Shirley, gave me the bagels and the lox. She gave me the menorah and the Chanukah gift. When she moved to Florida, it was a card with a twenty-dollar bill stuck inside. Her kitchen smelled of kugel and sable. It smelled of brisket and sadness. She was not a very actualized woman unless being a matriarch was her goal. If it was her goal, she was quite actualized. Her kitchen—whether on Ocean Avenue, Sheepshead Bay, in Brooklyn or Fort Lauderdale in Florida—was the holy space. I suppose this is an old story. The assimilation story. The High Holidays always meant something, but they didn't really mean something even though they were everything. They meant that you had to never forget you were a Jew no matter how you experienced them. Shirley's High Holidays, her Passover seders, her Purim, were always just about the food. The control of the food. There was so much joy in her chicken soup but there was so much salt that you couldn't help but be present.

Hineni.

Every Shabbat, after the chicken has been cooked, the candles placed, the sides deposited into their white, ceramic bowls, I place the challah on its wooden board, and right before I cover it, my favorite part, I sprinkle the salt. The salt is my favorite part. To dip. The sorrow. The difficulty. The pain. I do not mean to romanticize a history filled with horror that we Jews have endured. I used to believe that there was a beauty in suffering. A younger me. And I do understand this when I want to disappear into those Rosh Hashanah autumn leaves. As I get older, though, it bothers me. There is nothing you can do about the past but see it, name it, make poems and songs from it, so you can hopefully find joy in even the most difficult aspects of what has gone before. But, really....? Was it all necessary in any shape or form?

In synagogue, especially this year, I find myself in tears. I am always crying. I have no idea why. The hostages. October 7th. America. Moses. The aleph. The shofar. I don't know and I really don't know. It's beyond me and I welcome it because it feels good and if feeling good is joy, not pleasure—something fleeting—then I am in. All the way in. *Hineni*. But it's a different *Hineni*. This is not the feeling I got in my grandmother's kitchen. It's not the feeling I got singing Joni Mitchell's "Both Sides Now" at the hippie, progressive, mainly Jewish summer camp in Wallkill, New York. It's not the feeling of living in New York as a kid, as a man in his 20s, knowing that the Jews were everywhere and that Brooklyn and Manhattan were home, filled with my people. I always loved that, but it wasn't this.

It was those trees.

Hineni.

I am here. I am going to pray, and I am going to pray in front of these windows, in front of these trees changing color, in their death, and I am here, inside the sorrow of all of it and this is a wildly mysterious element of my Jewishness as an older person that is an absolute joy of my Judaism. I am in it.

Hineni.

Once, a few years back, I got a job at Maimonides School, teaching middle school English, in Brookline. I was hired by a man named Dov Huff. I sat in his office waiting for him to interview me and thought, *What the hell am I doing here?* I knew nothing from Modern Orthodox Jews. Dov and I talked. We laughed. We spoke of music. He was very present and engaged. He had a guitar in his office, and he hired me. I worked at Maimonides for two years and it was the best two years I ever spent at a school because there was so much joy in that place, I didn't know what to do with it. So, I just stood in it, lived in it, taught in it, walked in it. I was the most secular shaft of light in that whole place, but those folks loved me, and I loved them. It was tribal and there was no judgement because they knew who they were and what they were about, and it was lived.

I asked Dov about this once—why he thought I felt so comfortable in a school where I was not Modern Orthodox. He replied, *Hineni*.

I replied, I don't know what that means. Please tell me.

You are here, he said, and smiled.

I was.

My grandmother would never understand because her kitchen was exclusionary. It doesn't matter. To be a Jew, I have come to realize, is the great experience of the sorrow in the joy and the joy in the sorrow. I wish every day was Rosh Hashanah. All the sweetness with the salt at the other end, after Yom Kippur, on the challah plate. But it can't be. But then again, it can. The big window, the trees of God and color and death and the magnificence. All you have to do is be here, be in it—the exuberance and exaltation and the constant anticipation of surprise.

Hineni.

My Art, My Song, My Prayer*
Aliza Marton

For me, there is no clear line between my artwork, my connection to God, and Jewish spirituality. My personal journey as an artist has been deeply shaped by the deserts—both literal and metaphorical—that my ancestors traversed.

My paternal grandfather arrived in the United States through Ellis Island in 1917. His mother, a young orphan, journeyed for months through Ukraine with her five children, enduring unimaginable hardships. One chilling story passed down through my family is of my great-uncle Sam, who fell out of a wheelbarrow as they trudged through the snow. The Cossacks who found him noticed he was circumcised and realized he must be Jewish. Miraculously, they returned him unharmed. Knowing the history of Cossack-led massacres, such as the Chmielnicki pogroms, this act of mercy feels nothing short of divine intervention.

Though naturally artistic, my grandfather never had the opportunity to pursue his talent. Yet, he passed the "art gene" to my father and his sisters, all of whom displayed remarkable creativity.

On my mother's side, the journey was vastly different but no less formative. Her Sephardic roots trace back to the Spanish Inquisition, where our ancestor Don Avraham Senior Coronel served as an advisor to King Ferdinand and Queen Isabella. Despite his position in the royal court, the expulsion of the Jews forced the family to flee. A remnant of their home still stands in Segovia, Spain, now a museum. Don Avraham is said to have funded Christopher Columbus—a Jew secretly fleeing persecution—but my ancestors moved on to Turkey, Syria, and eventually Egypt, where my mother was born.

In 1956, when Nasser rose to power, Jews were no longer welcome in Egypt. My mother's family spent months in a refugee camp in Italy before being relocated to a tiny two-bedroom apartment in Rio de Janeiro, where seven people awaited U.S. visas for ten years.

It was in Brazil that my mother discovered her artistic gift. Using discarded chalk left behind by schoolchildren, she began to carve and draw, unknowingly launching a lifelong passion for sculpture. Later, after settling in California, my grandmother also began to paint, leaving us with beautiful works to treasure.

I grew up knowing of the hardships my family endured, but no one spoke much about art. Was art something that could only thrive when life's storms had calmed?

I am reminded of our Jewish ancestors' artistic endeavor in the desert after surviving our first great storm. When our people were freed from Egypt, they built the Mishkan. Despite their lack of formal training, their artistry in weaving tapestries, crafting the menorah, and gilding the ark was breathtaking because it came from the heart, an outpouring of gratitude to God.

I believe God grants each of us unique gifts, and one day, we will stand before Him to account for how we used them. Yet how many of us remain unaware of these gifts or let them lay dormant? I am so grateful I discovered mine.

Growing up, I struggled to find my place. My school didn't offer art classes, and my dyslexia and other learning challenges often left me feeling lost. I doodled incessantly—in notebooks, on walls, and even on my clothing—but my artistic endeavors were dismissed as a waste of time, more vandalism than creativity. By the time I reached college, I had nearly forgotten I once had a dream of becoming an artist. Life progressed, and that dream faded into the background. I embraced my roles as wife and mother, finding fulfillment in nurturing my family. Creativity peeked through in small ways—teaching children, cooking elaborate meals—but the artist within me seemed to slip further away.

While I thought my chance had passed, I wanted to give my children the opportunity to express themselves freely through art—something I was never allowed to do. As soon as they were able, I enrolled my girls in art classes. I was so proud of their paintings. We always framed and hung them up in our home. When I would pick up my girls after class, the teacher would always ask me, "When are *you* going to start painting?" Although she planted that seed, the idea felt selfish. Could I really paint for myself? Everyone had always said "no."

Finally, I mustered the courage and asked if I could join the class. When I sat beside my twelve-year-old daughter, a spark reignited within me. I felt like I was stepping into a vibrant, sacred world. Everywhere I looked, I saw God—in the intricate veins of leaves, the curve of a branch, the endless sky, and even in the chaos of my laundry pile, which seemed to multiply like manna from heaven!

My first painting was of a man praying at the Kotel, inscribed with the words *Hodu Lashem Ki Tov Ki L'Olam Chasdo.* (Give thanks to God, for He is good; His kindness is eternal.) I was overwhelmed with gratitude—for the ability to create, to see the world with wonder, and to connect with God through my art. I often found myself inspired by biblical passages, particularly Psalms, weaving them into my paintings.

I was always a little introverted, more internal by nature, but as I continued on this path, the paint became my voice; the easel, my stage; the brushes—my song!

My art has become more than an artistic expression. It is a form of prayer—a way to honor the beauty of creation and the resilience of those who came before me. Like my ancestors, I strive to craft something meaningful, reflecting the gifts God has given me. Through every brushstroke and every color, I feel a profound connection to Him and gratitude for the blessings in both the mundane and the miraculous. Everything our Jewish ancestors did for God formed a root character trait within us, lying dormant, waiting to be awakened to serve Him. My sincere hope is that when people see my art, the Godly spark within them is ignited.

*The cover art for *Manna Songs* is "Day 7—Shabbat" from my collection titled titled "Days of Creation." The painting symbolizes the completion of Creation. God showed us, by example, that Creation was not complete without a day of rest.

Identity in My Daily Cup

Lynne Golodner

The crystals swirl in hot water, little bubbles foaming on the surface. I add some milk and gulp it down while it's warm. I never finish a whole cup, but memories bubble up in the brew, which is why I keep buying the red can from a dusty grocery shelf half a world away from where it was made.

No one in my house drinks the same coffee as I do, Elite brand instant, straight from Israel. I drink it not for the taste but for the memory.

Did I really want that cup of instant coffee when I was young and in Israel for the first time? I was a journalist at a weekly newspaper, brought to the Jewish state by *Sar-El*, Volunteers for Israel, to write articles about their program of putting tourists on Army bases to build a connection with land and legacy. Two weeks of twisting wires on the Golan Heights to help gird bunkers for soldiers, I slept in a dank barracks with four others, where the wind howled at night and a coal stove burned smelly in the corner of the room. The shower was a spigot with cold water raining down, and I endured it all because I was young and adventurous.

One Shabbat I spent in the Old City, in a hostel for single young women who were playing with the idea of becoming religious. It was there that I drank Elite for the first time.

A metal urn sat on a folding table in the lobby, a can of Elite instant coffee beside it, with Styrofoam cups and plastic spoons and powdery artificial creamer and a small cup of sugar. I swirled the brown crystals into the hot water. Bitter and strong, this particular coffee sat on kitchen shelves in most Israeli homes, but few people drank it. By sipping local coffee, I believed I could taste the sweat of my ancestors and the dust of this hard-won land that accepted me exactly as I am.

"You like that?" a young woman asked. She wore a skirt to the floor and long sleeves, simple gold earrings and no makeup.

I nodded. The taste reminded me of quiet nights and whispered prayers, things I'd learned in the homes of strangers who followed the rules of the religious and invited me to try. A woman who tugged at her long brown wig and held a baby on her lap while four older children ran around the table and her husband chanted the blessings. A rabbi's wife who danced with the Torah in her arms as if it were a precious child, eyes closed, her body humming with the spirit of tradition. A couple, high school sweethearts long married, who blessed their grown daughter in quiet whispers on Friday night. I was only just beginning to know the rich history of my ancestors, wondering if I was cut out for a life more religious than the one I'd been raised in.

We lit tea lights, waving the flame toward us and singing the prayer aloud, familiar from childhood Fridays with my grandparents. Then we walked quick along stone alleyways, a human river rushing down steep steps to the Western Wall as the sun sank low and the night glimmered. The young women from the hostel were newly religious and excited about bringing more of us into the fold. Their skirts swept against the cold stones.

We pushed past metal detectors turned off for the Sabbath and pressed into the women's section, swaying beside scarf-wrapped heads and prayer-closed eyes. After, I joined dozens of twentysomethings for dinner at the gleaming apartment of an American couple. The conversation ran thick with contempt for less observant ways. Was the price of becoming religious turning your back on family? Eager young people with a toe already in the murky waters of religion boasted about abandoning superficial childhoods to embrace the richness of Torah. Young women proudly choosing denim skirts over short shorts dreamt of marrying pious young men. *They're brainwashed*, I thought, wondering if they believed everything they said, wondering if they'd grow bored, tired, resentful some years down the line, too afraid to turn back. *How can they insult the parents who loved them?* I pictured my mother and father in Michigan, hearing their *I love you* at the end of every call.

But Israel—and religion—was a different kind of home for me, a place I belonged the first time I stepped on the dry, fragrant earth. And the scent of that coffee—chestnut and soil, like the forest floor itself—was another kind of homecoming.

At the hostel, I slept on a creaking bunkbed in a dormitory room with five other women on the second floor of an old stone building. The walls were cold, but the rooms warm with the flurry of conversation. The mattress was thin, and the springs groaned under my body as I shifted in the night.

The next day, I ate sweet, sticky *yerushalmi* kugel in the home of an old rabbi. His disciples bragged that it was the old man who made the kugel, not his wife. It went down easy. Relegated to a side room with the women, I leaned toward the rabbi's voice, straining for familiar words in his Hebrew sermon. The coffee was everywhere, hot and ready, a constant flavor at every table.

Eventually, I embraced Orthodoxy, but I only stayed in that world for ten years. Still, I love stopping for Shabbat. Halting all doing, no running here and there, a day away from checking items off my ever long list. I no longer stay up late on Thursdays to cook, but I still invite people to my Friday table to sit long in quiet conversation and sing the words of our souls.

Shabbat taught me to notice. To listen well. To see the lavender fingers of evening groping toward the night. To pay attention to words and find meaning that resonates over time.

Good-natured debate over coffee and cake. Singing, full-throated and resonant, like bells in a walled city, palms pounding the fine wood of my table, reverberations felt by everyone around it.

I've been buying Elite instant coffee for more than thirty years. A few stores in my town carry it, but often I order three cans at a time direct from Israel. I drink more tea than coffee these days, but when I find the need to reconnect with my soul, I pull out that red can, stir two teaspoonfuls into hot water and watch the memories foam.

I've lived many shades of Jewish, and this daily cup remains a constant, an anchor as I shift and change. Its taste familiar, something I recognize no matter what happens in the wider world, or in me as I age. I like the taste of it now. It took time, like all good things. Like a strong identity. Sometimes I don't even need the milk.

When I sip from my cup, I taste my own innocence, hear the echo of quick steps on stone paths reverberating off the tall walls of an old city. I was young then, and searching, and I swear, when I drink this coffee, I am once again that girl, open and eager, uncertain about what will come, but confident that it will be good.

Pass the Peas
Adrienne Dern

The message was loud, if not clear. From my parents' perspective, our family's Jewish identity was essential to who we were. It evoked both pride and fear, but the missing piece, never fully articulated, was the "why."

I hadn't given this much thought. There was no reason to. But something called me to read Philip Roth's *The Plot Against America* and it began to unearth what lay beneath the surface.

I wasn't prepared for it. Published in 2004, the story goes like this: It's 1940 and FDR loses what would have been his third term as President to Charles Lindbergh, an aviation hero and confirmed antisemite. Although a novel, the story carries the names of Roth's own family, including the narrator, a boy aged seven to nine, named Philip Roth.

The book rocked my world.

Roth was 18 years older than me. Over the years 1940-1942, during which *The Plot Against America* takes place, my mother would have been a pre-teen, my dad in his teens. Like Roth's family, they lived through World War II and the Holocaust from a safe perch in New Jersey. But unlike in Roth's fictional family, but I'm guessing also in his real one, these events were not discussed in mine.

The awareness of antisemitism sits front-and-center in the book; in my life, in the background. Even so, its impact was felt, starting with the imperative that one day I would marry a Jewish man.

My high school friends and I headed to New York City, excited to see *Fiddler on the Roof* on Broadway. Again, I was unprepared. As the story unfolds, Chava, the youngest of the three daughters, flouts tradition to marry the non-Jewish love of her life and is swiftly disowned. Was this to be my fate? My tears were unstoppable as we made our way to Chinatown for dinner, imagining my own future, cast aside by my parents.

Of course, that didn't happen, and five years later when I announced that I would marry Mark, the non-Jewish love of my life, my mother's initial response was this: "I always knew you would marry someone just like your father." Her second comment, a question, really, and one I thought was getting ahead of the situation, was this: "How will you raise your children?"

That turned out to be a moot question as we divorced six-and-a-half years later without progeny. But it underscored the message of sticking with the clan. Ironically, I'd venture to say that my parents preferred Mark to my second husband who was Jewish.

In fifth grade our teacher sent us home with a question: "Where was our family from?" Seemed simple enough, but it wasn't. Again, my mother: "We're Jewish so we're American." I was ashamed to arrive without an answer like "Italy" or "Ireland." Although we never hid our Jewish identity, it must have been that Poland or Russia felt potentially dangerous, identifying us as a family whose ancestors were Jews forced to flee Eastern Europe.

That may explain why my paternal grandfather, my only grandparent born outside the U.S., changed the family name from Derishinsky to Dern when my dad was in utero.

Roth's story was packed with familiar references to my own life. Towns near where I grew up; the Studebaker driven by his family and mine; a family trip to Washington, D.C., where both of our fathers, daunted by one of the city's many traffic circles, had to be safely escorted around the circle by a friendly cop; shopping at Bamberger's department store, and an anecdote about getting locked in a bathroom, although the circumstances were different—one on the ground, one in the air.

Beyond the Jewish elements of his story, reading Roth helped me understand the absence of deep discussion on any subject in my family. I laughed when I recently heard the actress Allison Janney describe dinner-table conversation in her family this way: "Pass the peas." So relatable. But then I wondered, "At what cost?"

I'm not here to blame my parents but to try to understand what this has meant in my life. Is this why I often take things at face value? Could I have become a more critical thinker? If I had had children, would I have done any better? What else weren't we talking about?

These are questions that haunt me now. But there are many others I didn't know I needed answers to before reading Roth's book. If I could have asked them before cancer and Alzheimer's claimed their lives, what would my parents have told me about the Jewish part of our story? And what difference would it have made?

While these questions linger, they don't diminish the pleasure I take in embracing my identity as a Jewish woman.

I happily recall—and occasionally use—Yiddish expressions, including some that are suspect, invented, I believe, by my dad. I wonder if there's ever been a more vivid language.

Celebrating Passover, marking Rosh Hashanah and breaking the Yom Kippur fast with friends is a delight. On Passover, I get a kick out of gentile guests who quietly pass on the gefilte fish when it's offered while happily devouring more familiar food, like brisket and noodle kugel. And a special shout-out to matzoh ball soup. It heals what ails any day of the year.

I observe with delight as my grandparent friends kvell with much-deserved pride at the bar and bat mitzvahs of their grandchildren. It's awe-inspiring to watch a 13-year-old do something I would struggle to do at 73.

Let's not forget the fun of "Jewish geography." I recently shook with delight as I pieced together a connection between my first cousin who lives in Maine and my local tech guru in Silver Spring, Maryland. All thanks to Jersey City!

Being Jewish can be complicated. But finding the pleasures offered by connection, language, food, and the intangible aspects of being part of this particular tribe are reasons enough to celebrate my Jewish identity. We get each other's jokes; there are things we don't have to explain; we know each other in our bones.

So, I take a seat at my kitchen table to share a plate of rugelach or mandel bread alongside friends with last names like Rabinovich, Schoenfeld and Goldberg. As I do, I thank Philip Roth for pushing me to more deeply consider the complexity of my Jewish heritage, from the denials and fears of my childhood to the appreciation of what being Jewish means to me today.

Living Without Doubt
Sarah Leibov

I have a secret almost no one knows. I'm not Jewish— not technically. I was unaware of this fact until I was twenty years old. My father's first cousin, who changed his name from Alan to Eli when he left Chicago for Israel, took it upon himself to tell me.

In the fall of 1996, I spent four months living on Kibbutz Ramat Rachel. There I was a participant in Project Oren, which provided programming for Jews from around the world to live and volunteer on kibbutzim while learning Hebrew.

Though I loved the friends I met there, and exploring nearby Jerusalem with them, I was homesick. I alleviated some of this by writing letters to my family in Chicago and by visiting Eli and his wife and five children in their home in the West Bank. He'd pick me up from the train station, and as we drove to the settlement where they lived, I'd spot the minarets of neighboring Arab villages along the way. I was wary of the gun he kept in the glove compartment, but my nerves calmed once we arrived safely in the gated community, where his wife would welcome me with hugs and cake. My younger cousins, who spoke no English despite their American father, attempted to communicate with me in spite of my rudimentary Hebrew.

Eli and his family tolerated my ignorance regarding their orthodox customs, such as the time I accidentally put a meat dish on the dairy side of the kitchen. I once tried to hug Eli, and he froze. My grandmother later told me that it was not allowed for religious men to hug women outside their immediate family.

His family took me on long walks around the neighborhood, showing me the shul where there were separate areas not only for women, but for

Ashkenazim and Sephardim. It was on one such walk that Eli recommended that I convert to Judaism.

"What do you mean?" I blinked at him, confused. "I am Jewish."

"You aren't," he stated. Eli was quiet, polite, and hid his expressions behind a long beard.

"Your mother didn't have a real conversion," he continued. "It was through a Reform rabbi. She didn't get in the mikveh. It doesn't count."

I was stunned that Eli was more familiar with the details concerning my mother's conversion than I was. Although I knew she had converted before she married my father, I also knew that her Judaism was—well—flexible. She served honey glazed ham and chocolate eggs on Easter, which I didn't particularly mind. However, I never questioned *my* Judaism. My parents made a point of telling me that my mother converted so that their children would be considered Jewish. She made sure my brother and I went to synagogue and Hebrew school until I refused to go and dropped out at the age of twelve.

My teenage years were marked by that same rebellion, and my time in Israel at the age of twenty was a choice I made to reconnect with an aspect of me that I had always held close, if not actively celebrated. Even if it was dormant, it was ever present. So, to be told that my Jewish identity was a falsehood came as a shock.

Filled with doubt, I told my father's other cousin, Nita, what Eli had said—that I needed to convert to Judaism. Nita had also grown up with my father and Eli in Chicago, and as a secular Zionist, had made Aliyah in her 20s. Now in her 40s, she lived in Jerusalem and taught at Hebrew University. She and Eli, diametrically opposed on politics and religion, hadn't spoken to each other in years. "That's bullshit," she scoffed. "Of course you're Jewish! Don't ever let anyone tell you that you're not—especially not him."

I stopped considering conversion, but Eli's words lit a fire in me that otherwise might not have been ignited. Realizing that others questioned my identity, I actively pursued Judaism. I had a bat mitzvah two months later at a Reform synagogue in Jerusalem to make up for the one I had rejected as a teen. When I returned to college in Chicago, I majored in international relations, with a focus on the history and politics of the Middle East. I continued studying Hebrew and picked up a minor in Jewish Studies. I joined Hillel and taught Sunday school at a local synagogue.

I spent my junior year abroad studying at Tel Aviv University, and when I returned to the States, my maternal grandfather took me aside. He told me that as a soldier in World War II, he served under a Jewish general, Maurice Rose, who was killed by the Nazis. Eleven days later, their unit, the 3rd Armored Division, entered a recently liberated Buchenwald. The men were stunned by the atrocities they found there. They took pictures and made copies for every single soldier so that no one could deny what had occurred there. My grandfather said that they also did this to honor General Rose, who did not live to see what had been done to his people.

My grandfather's hands shook as he showed me the nineteen black and white photos. They depicted a microcosm of what he had witnessed—numerous naked skeletons carelessly piled on top of one another in rubble, alongside the starved, emaciated survivors dressed in striped prison uniforms. General Eisenhower, who visited Buchenwald at the same time, was so shocked by what he saw that he ordered German civilians be brought in to witness the horrors the Nazis perpetuated. It was my grandfather's job to pick up nearby villagers and to drive them into the concentration camp and make them look at what they had denied.

My grandfather showed me the photos in 1999, almost 55 years after he left Germany, but the grief he felt as an American soldier in Buchenwald was still very present. He told me a few more stories before giving me the photos for safekeeping. This was the moment the two branches of my family converged—my non-Jewish grandfather lovingly passing off this part of his history, ensuring its safety to his Jewish granddaughter.

I took the pictures to Hillel and shared them with survivors from Buchenwald who came to speak to the students a few months later. I was surprised that instead of being upset, they appreciated that I had brought the photos and even recognized some of the people in them. When the Illinois Holocaust Museum opened in Skokie a few years later, I donated copies of the photos for them to display.

Though I felt my Jewish identity was settled, Eli wasn't the last one to try to tell me I wasn't Jewish, or not Jewish enough. When I returned from studying in Israel, a boyfriend told me his parents didn't consider me to be Jewish because my family didn't keep kosher. Recently I told my husband, who was born to two Jewish parents, that a friend said I was the least Jewish person she knows because we don't belong to a synagogue. He laughed and told me that I am the most Jewish person he knows.

My husband and I know something these people do not. My Jewish identity is not dependent on adhering to a rule system, but on integrating Judaism into my life in a manner that feels authentic to me. There are so many ways to celebrate my identity and to be able to share those aspects of myself with my family, friends, and community. Whether I am cooking traditional recipes, teaching my students about the holidays, or advocating for Jewish genetic screening, I get to decide what makes me feel blessed and fulfilled as a Jew, and no one can take that away. My history and ancestry are complex, an inheritance of both blessing and trauma, and my Jewish pride encompasses it all. I honor both sides of my family when I speak about the injustice that has happened (and continues to happen) to Jews.

A few months after the Hamas massacre of innocent Israeli civilians on October 7th, I attended a Hanukkah vigil for the victims where we prayed for the safe return of the hostages and lit the candles. I felt then that our faith is about finding light in the darkness and holding out for hope—this is how we have survived as a people. There isn't room for judgment among a people who take up so little physical space in the world, who have been under attack for thousands of years, to tell others that they are not allowed at the table. I no longer question my Judaism, and I don't care what other people think about it either. My hope is that all Jews, regardless of their backgrounds, find a way to come together, to celebrate and uphold our mutual heritage, and to fight those who seek to destroy us.

When a Norwegian Converts to Judaism: The Viking Bar Mitzvah and Other Adventures in Jewish Joy

Nina B. Lichtenstein

Helmets with horns on every table: check. Big plastic swords decorating walls: check. Five varieties of homemade herring on the buffet: check. Homemade gravlaks sliced and ready for 250 guests: check. Aquavit and shot glasses on the "adult" beverage table: check.

I wipe my hands on the long, white chef's apron tied around my waist, protecting my flowing, maxi, off-white skirt, and long-sleeved wrap-around top, as my gaze wanders to the wall-mounted clock in our *shul*'s social hall. Time for me to join the others in the sanctuary—family and friends from near and far, our regular congregants always included in each other's simchas, and best of all, my firstborn son, 13-year-old Tobias, about to be bombarded by the iconic "Daim," individually wrapped, fun-sized Norwegian candy, as soon as he finishes the last blessing over his Haftorah portion.

I have been Jewish since I was twenty-three, and in this moment, I am a forty-three-year-old veteran Jew-by-Choice, who has joyfully embraced all the practices of a modern orthodox life in suburban East Coast America. Except, you can take the girl out of Norway, but you can't take Norway out of the girl. A funny thing happened when I immigrated to the U.S. and converted to Judaism: As my Jewish identity rooted itself in my muscle memory and viscera, my emotional memory simmered on a slow fire, stoking my nostalgia for all things Norwegian and, perhaps, also for my Norwegian identity itself, which had ceded way to my newfound *yiddishkeit* on steroids.

I lived in Norway from birth until the age of nineteen when I left for the States with a gap-year plan; then, "just a year" turned into forty before

I knew it. I was not brought up with much tradition, and certainly not with any of Norway's cultural tradition of Christian Lutheranism. In fact, raised in Oslo as a latchkey kid with what today would be considered way too much freedom (to get in trouble, to get hurt), I must have yearned for what the observant Jewish life I later immersed myself in would provide: rules, framework, tradition, predictability, clear parameters for yes and no, can and can't, should and shouldn't. And lots of homecooked, festive meals. I loved my life as a Jewish woman, then wife, then mother. I thrived as I had found my happy place, my meaningful, existential purpose.

My three sons were (of course) all circumcised, went to Jewish day school from nursery through 8th grade, have Jewish names like Tuvia Yaakov, Gavriel Nadav, and Benyamin Reu'el. For the first 14 years of their lives, they wore *kippot* and *tztitzit*, and if one of them picked up a pair of scissors or a marker on Shabbat, the others would yell, "*Moktsah! Moktsah!*" trained as they had been at school and at home about steering clear of forbidden activities on the day of rest. They played the best together on Shabbat when electronics were off the table and they had to be creative and collaborative in making their fun, and I involved them in Shabbat and holiday preparations so that they could take ownership in the outcome: our special times together celebrating Jewish traditions, joyfully. In essence, I gave them everything I did not have growing up, and I believe they are happy for it.

But I also wanted my sons to experience Norwegian joy, and so they went to summer camps in Norway (where they were the only circumcised boys), bringing their own kosher hotdogs and marshmallows for the campfire. When we lived in Norway for a year when they were in elementary and middle school, they experienced the ultimate immersion in all things Norwegian. But when attending their weekly cheider classes at the Oslo *shul*, they got to be fully Jewish *and* fully Norwegian with their peers. With their über-traditional Norwegian and Viking middle-names of Thor, Balder, and Odin, they still love to rap in Norwegian while their silver Magen Davids and Thor's hammer necklaces dangle around their necks. They are my joyful Viking Jewish boychiks.

The Lichtenstein Viking bar mitzvah became somewhat of a legend in our *shul* and community, and to this day folks talk to me not just about the food ("How many kinds of herring did you make, again?") but also recall the little trolls, the lush, green chunks of moss, granite-colored rocks, and speckled white birch branches that decorated the tables, all reminiscent of my beloved motherland. On every special occasion, including the weekly celebration of Shabbat, I infuse some Norwegian spirit if I can. For example, when I bake challah, I add a teaspoon of cardamon to the dough, as this is a classic Scandinavian way to make sweet and yeasty baked goods. When my father died in 2012, and I wanted to mark the *shloshim* in some way that honored him even though he was not Jewish, I made my gravlaks and brought it with a bottle of Aquavit to the *se'utdat shlishit* in *shul*, sharing stories of him with the intimate and mostly older male group—his contemporaries—gathered for that final light meal before *havdallah*.

Although traditional Ashkenazi and Eastern European cuisine has quite a bit in common with my native Scandinavian dietary traditions (herring, potatoes, smoked fish in all varieties), and I have become a pro at dishing up kugels, chicken soup, and brisket, it is Sephardi and Mizrahi recipes and spices (essentially what we consider Israeli /Middle Eastern food) that I have enjoyed adapting into my own cooking repertoire the most. When I am back home in Norway for visits, I love nothing more than to prepare meals for family and friends that incorporate the flavors, textures, and colors of a lamb rubbed and roasted with *ras el-hanout*, Moroccan carrot and beet salad, babaganoush, or the sweet *malabi* milk pudding made with rose water and topped with velvety, red pomegranate sauce. In Norway, sharing my Jewish traditions —food or holiday related—has been a source of pride and joy for me.

Ten years ago, I moved from Connecticut to Maine, where my homesickness indicator for Norway went from a steady eight to a two, in no small part due to the geography and climate so reminiscent of the land where I grew up. With its scarce one million inhabitants, this huge northern state has a surprisingly active and diverse Jewish community, with many synagogues and temples, and Chabad Houses, too. I no longer live according to strict Orthodox rules, but enjoy new-found ways to express Jewish joy, while also staying true to most traditional Jewish observances. For example, on Sukkot, our "Viking Sukkah" is my way of creating a unique Jewish *hygge* experience for our guests with huge, warm, sheepskins on every chair, making sure that even here in the north, where fall evening temperatures can dip into the 40s, we stay cozy.

There is a reason I have come to call myself "The Viking Jewess." The title represents the hybrid and joyful self that I have become: a distinctive blend of everything I carry with me from my Norwegian heritage, combined with all the beauty, traditions, and flavors of my Jewish identity. A Jewish woman at almost sixty years old who herself never had a bat mitzvah, I wonder if preparing for my own, albeit belated, rite of passage could be a meaningful goal for my next decade. And while I may not go wild with swords and helmets with horns, I might incorporate some ice-bathing or a buffet of (very stinky) fermented trout: some Viking ways to exhilarate the senses of my guests while celebrating Jewish joy with me.

On Jewish Life in Spain
Julia Grunes

In Spain, the places where Jews gather are kept secret. Living Jews, that is. Anyone can find the locations of the old Jewish Quarters, can wander down those streets with the aid of €2 pamphlets, can walk through the few emptied synagogues. In Toledo, tour guides brag about the *Sinagoga de Santa María la Blanca*, which they claim is the oldest synagogue structure still standing in Europe.

There are little educational museums that tell you how those old, mystical Jews lived. The holidays they celebrated, the clothes they wore, the *shofars* and *tallit* they used. In Segovia's *Centro Didáctico de la Judería*, they even have a model of what the main synagogue used to look like, complete with blue-white holograms going through the motions of a Saturday morning service again and again and again at the whim of tourists.

I spent a long time watching the model, watching those hologram-Jews. Maybe I felt some joy at hearing these familiar songs, the songs that served as background while my friends and I crawled under chairs during *b'nai mitzvahs*, stealing candies, the songs that I harmonized with before I even understood what harmonizing was.

But maybe I felt something else too. A sort of numbness, at those hologram-Jews, at those songs, carefully contained behind glass and what the *Centro Didáctico* refers to as "cutting-edge information technology media." At how far away it all seemed to be. In spite of that, those hologram-Jews are there always to be looked at and listened to—at least during visiting hours.

Living Jews, though. They're a bit more difficult to pin down.

Difficult, even though I'm currently based in Madrid, which, along with Barcelona, houses the most Jews currently living in Spain. But I found a temple online that has services on Friday nights and after explaining my situation, sending in my passport picture, and answering questions about my congregation in New York, I was given the address.

Pretty much all the spaces where living Jews gather in Spain—at least the ones I've seen—don't list their location on their website. It made me feel as if Spain's Jewish community was as far away as those hologram-Jews in Segovia. Maybe even further, actually, because these Jews were hidden behind something far less transparent than glass.

I had made it over the biggest hurdle though—I had an address. It was to a nondescript building, and if the security guards hadn't been outside, I would've been sure that I had been given the wrong one. But I had been warned about the security guards, told that I was on their list, and after stumbling through an explanation of who I was in barely passable Spanish, I was allowed inside.

It's hard to explain the way I felt that Friday night. It isn't as if I'm the most regular participant in Friday night services in my temple at home. But, surrounded by other Jews singing עושה שלום, the prayer for peace, in the same tune we used at my temple in New York, it was as if something in me uncoiled. It was as if I could breathe for the first time since I had arrived in Spain.

I think it was then that I realized how much my Judaism had been this tight, clenching *thing* in my chest.

Because Jewish life is quiet here, contained. It's hidden in buildings that look like any other, the clear antithesis of the cathedrals that tower over the streets. It's hidden in Kosher stores without shop signs, in carefully guarded WhatsApp groups, in posters for events that never have an address.

It's vastly different from how I grew up as a Jew in Monroe, New York, where there are not only reform and conservative synagogues, but a Chabad as well. Monroe also sits directly next to Kiryas Joel, a village made up of Satmar Hasidic Jews. Their signs are written in Yiddish and their clothes mark them as Jewish in a way that I have never marked myself.

I was surrounded by Jewish life growing up, but it wasn't a constant. I was still always the minority in school, the one explaining Jewish holidays and culture to those who asked. And then, in college, this was amplified as I interacted with people who had never met a Jewish person before.

But I have never felt the way I did, the way that I do now, in Spain. I never thought that I could be so excited at the tiniest sign of Jewish life. Of a kippah, of a promise of a "New York style bagel," of a siddur.

I never thought I could feel a crackling sort of connection at the sight of a swastika on a metro platform.

To clarify, the swastika was crossed out, an arrow pointing to it and a *fuck you!* hanging on to the end of it. When I first saw it, I could barely stop myself from tracing my fingers over the arrow. That succinct *fuck you!* felt important. I felt indelibly linked to whoever wrote it. Maybe they were Jewish. Maybe they weren't. But they were with me, with us, regardless, and that made me feel a little bit less alone.

In my search for Jewish life here, I have started to look for pieces like that—not swastikas, but little things, little moments—that make me feel less alone. I won't claim that I've found a Jewish community in which I feel at home, but I have found pieces, and for now, those pieces are enough.

Pieces like watching the *Prince of Egypt* on Passover at four in the morning, drunk off Chabad wine with a couple of friends, finding comfort with each other since we couldn't be home for the seders. Bringing interested non-Jewish friends to Shabbat dinners to talk and eat and laugh and tell stories about the way I celebrate with my own family. Sitting on the floor in my room with my Jewish roommate and laughing while we talk about our trauma responses, because there is nothing we can do but laugh.

These pieces, to me, create a far more realistic picture of Jewish life than any abandoned Jewish Quarter or well-meaning museum ever could. I'm not saying that these pieces represent Jewish life in Spain as a whole. They represent my life, though, one that is far less serious and regimented than the life of the hologram-Jews found in Segovia's *Centro Didáctico de la Judería*.

Each Jewish person I have met in Spain contributes to and interacts with Judaism differently, mixing the traditional with the modern, finding their own place in the little pockets of Jewish community scattered throughout the country. And these Jewish communities are here, *we* are here, in Spain, even if the living Jews seem to be constantly overshadowed by the history of the dead ones. The communities are patchworks of Ashkenazi and Sephardic Jews, of temporary and permanent residents, of descendants of *conversos*, but they are here.

It's important to remember the history of Judaism in Spain. It's a large part of why Jewish life in Spain is what it is today. But in remembering that history, space must also be made for the Jews that are living.

If that space isn't created, then what is the point of remembering at all?

How Shall I Hang My Mezuzah?
Eileen Vorbach Collins

Married under a chuppah by the cantor of the Reform synagogue my husband's family had belonged to for decades, I'd not given much thought to conversion. A few years later, pregnant with our first child, the idea took root. I wanted this as much for my children as for myself. It didn't matter to my husband, who thought the kids should decide when they were older. I opted for conversion, Reform style. My in-laws gave me a beautiful gold pendant inscribed with my new Hebrew name and signed on the back, *Love, Mom and Dad.* That was the first time I knew in my bones that it felt right.

A few years later, every mother in my playgroup had enrolled their precious progeny in preschool. I didn't see the point since I'd be home with the new baby anyway. I don't remember why I changed my mind. Maybe I simply wanted to fit in.

My husband, who'd early in our marriage convinced me to try a raw oyster, had quite abruptly become interested in following a more observant path. It was hard to keep up with his ever-escalating level of observance. There didn't seem to be much middle ground on which we both could rest, but together we decided to enroll our daughter in preschool two mornings a week at a nearby Conservative synagogue.

She was so excited, my independent three-year-old. While other kids snuggled in their mother's laps at Gymboree, Lydia wanted to be the instructor's assistant. On the long-awaited first day, my friend's son screamed and clung to his mother, his face an alarming vermilion as she pried his fingers from her flesh with help from the teacher. Lydia marched in without a backward glance— ready to take charge.

Even as my friend looked embarrassed by her son's neediness, I was besieged by insecurity. Had I failed to bond with this child who could leave me so easily? There must be some happy middle ground.

As soon as I got sweet good-natured baby Daniel home and in for a nap it would be time to get him up and strapped into the car seat to go and pick up Lydia. Preschool, overall, was a pain in the ass, but she looked forward to going, happily singing *"Dovid Melech Israel, chai, chai v'kayam"* over and over until the tune wormed its way into my brain and I found myself silently humming it during sex. It had a satisfying pattern of accelerating rhythm.

One day, early in her pre-school career, we were having lunch and I asked, "Lydia, how was school today?" She replied, "When I'm a boy I can wear a kippah."

And just when will you be a boy? I wondered.

At snack time the boys all donned their delightfully ornate Superman or Cookie Monster yarmulkes. For the more serious Talmudic toddler, there were elaborate Star of David motifs or iconic Holy Land scenes designed by artist Yair Emanuel, hand embroidered on velvet or raw silk in his studio in Jerusalem.

These yarmulkes were so beautiful you wanted to reach out and run your fingers over the threads. You had to keep yourself from gently lifting them off the little round heads and sniffing to see if they carried the scent of the desert. You wouldn't even be tempted to peek inside to check the label to see if they were authentic—you could just tell. I'd need to get my hands on one of those for my special child. I'd ask around. For now, one of her father's plain black ones would have to do.

The earnest young pre-school teacher patiently explained, "But women don't wear kippahs." I pointed out that my three-year-old was not a woman and that handing out the kippahs to boys was akin to having a party where only some guests got to wear the festive hats. Finally, after my persistent and bothersome arguments got me nowhere, I said it might be better to simply let my child play at home wearing whatever costume she chose. The administration acquiesced. Lydia could wear her coveted kippah. It seems silly now, but my rationale for fighting the kippah war was my conviction that a child should not be denied something based on gender. Lydia didn't have to keep waiting to become a boy.

I wasn't doing a great job of fitting in. There were many more pressing issues that would later surface, and I'd need to learn to pick my battles. We'd chosen this preschool for its proximity to our home, and because friends had recommended it. I hadn't considered how the level of religious observance might not align with my own values.

My husband, though, was now studying with an Orthodox rabbi at the nearby yeshiva. Our bookshelves sagged under the weight of the tomes he brought home.

By the time our children were three and five years old, we'd separated. My husband had moved to a community within the eruv. He no longer drove or turned on a light on Shabbos. His beard grew long, his payes bobbed, a kosher mezuzah graced his every doorpost. Divorce is hard for most children. Traveling between homes is unsettling. For our children, it meant rotating not only homes, but cultures.

My husband and I were still friends. We'd not initiated divorce proceedings. After two years apart, in a misguided attempt to reunite our family, I suggested we try again to be married and agreed to his condition that I convert "for real."

I could adapt. How hard could it be? We would be a family again. Our children were still young. They would get used to the change. They were already familiar with the neighborhood and had some friends there.

It wasn't as easy as I anticipated. My daughter had long ago given up her fleeting desire to wear a traditional men's head covering. Now she didn't want to wear a dress, resulting in tears and arguments. My son couldn't turn off the lights in his light-up sneakers on Shabbos earning him jeers of *Muktzeh Boy* from the neighborhood's bullies.

There was a lot of tension. A lot of heartache. A world of hurt all around. I'd been disenfranchised from my Protestant Sunday school upbringing by the hypocrisy of the church. I'd converted to Judaism not to embrace a new and better religion; I wasn't so naïve to think there might not be more of the same. I converted because I loved the traditions that were a part of my husband's family gatherings. I wanted that for my children. The feeling of belonging. Of lovely linen challah covers, serving platters with symbolic etchings, and exotic, embroidered tallit opening them to the mystery of prayer. The possibility, not the predictability, of God.

My second conversion, the mikvah, the quest to fit in. None of it worked. Despite having been found a credible candidate by the bet din, I was now the biggest hypocrite of all. I'd been an agnostic but hopeful convert. Our family was not reunited, we just all lived in the same house. Within two years we ended our marriage, no longer friends.

Lydia dyed her hair blue, pierced body parts, curated an eccentric wardrobe from thrift store finds, and created beautiful, disturbing works of art. She wasn't fitting in either. She also began a pattern of self harm that ended tragically in suicide when she was fifteen.

A few years later, Daniel's high school steel drum band was invited to play at the same Conservative synagogue where Lydia had attended preschool. At least half of the women wore not only lovely kippahs, but stunning prayer shawls. Women claiming this, making it their own. taking from tradition what felt right and holy.

Smiling at the evidence that my child had been ahead of her time, I wished she could have been there to see these women. Women who would sing to the Lord a new song. I imagined her small frame swaying, rocking on her heels, on her toes, wrapped in a fringed tallit with all the colors of the rainbow. The rough linen shroud we buried her in was so drab, so unlike her. I want her soul to soar.

There's a story about the common practice of hanging a mezuzah at a 45-degree angle. Two rabbis couldn't agree (surprise) about whether the placement should be horizontal or vertical. After much discussion, they reached a compromise. I wish our children could have found that middle ground that we, their parents, could not. The place they belong, where the history of their ancestors left its mark on their cells. The place that feels like home.

The place that for me, often feels like Brigadoon. A mysterious place where some are born, others happen across in their travels and are immediately home, while others, like me, will forever try to find their way back through a forest of memory and longing, never really knowing if it was ever ours to claim.

I Am a Jewish Poet
Robbi Nester

Every year, at my uncle's seder, I played the part of the simple child, who didn't know enough to ask the requisite questions. I sat through seders and services without knowing their substance. No one offered to explain them, and I didn't know how to ask. Both my parents grew up in observant homes and were committed Zionists at one time, who fought in the Israeli War of Independence and thought that they would make a life there. They each came independently to Israel, sharing the same dream, and helped to build a country. But the partisan battles of the stakeholders in this new nation and the harsh reality of warfare they faced shook their former faith in the idea of a Jewish state.

Each of them, my mother in the South African Air Force and my father in the American one, had participated in a World War that ranged across huge swaths of land and sky. That war had been a life-or-death battle for their own continued existence, but close combat in this tiny parcel of land claimed by two peoples made my parents profoundly uncomfortable, as their own families had so recently been forced to flee their homes to escape persecution.

My parents moved to my father's native country, the U.S., where they became quite openly skeptical about both religion and the state of Israel, though they still donated to a host of charities benefitting its people. They did not keep kosher or belong to any synagogue. As a teenager and young adult, I found that no one among my observant family members or in any other Jewish spaces filled in the blanks, teaching me what I had missed. Not having a Jewish education made me a perpetual outsider.

I didn't even have a bat mitzvah until I was 50, but I never let go of my Jewishness, even if shame at my ignorance kept me from learning more about it. I kept looking for a community that would allow me to find a kind of home.

As a child, I did attend religious school for a short while. In fact, learning the Hebrew alphabet made such an impact on me that when I went to the eye doctor for my yearly checkup, I read the chart from right to left without at first realizing my mistake.

It wasn't just the language either. At that time, prayer was still permitted in public schools, like the one in the Jewish suburb of Philadelphia I attended. The teachers were careful to select only passages from the Tanakh and Psalms in English translation, and I remember thinking how beautiful they were.

Yet I saw that my parents, my father particularly, did not really want to continue sending me to Hebrew school when he did not have the money to spend on a big bat mitzvah like the ones other girls in my neighborhood were having, so when he asked whether I wanted to continue my Jewish education, I said no. I opted instead to join a Jewish youth group and to go to holiday services with my friends at a nearby synagogue.

Though my father avoided involvement in organized religion, I realize now that I got my attachment to Jewish tradition through him. At the end of every work week, he stopped off at the bookstore and bank, picked up a book for me, and a shiny silver dollar. He let me drop the coin into a piggy bank and read me the book. I loved to hear him turn the letters into tales, a trick I could not wait to learn myself.

When I went to services on the high holidays, seders, and occasionally, Purim, I listened carefully to the words, even though I didn't know their exact meaning. I heard them often enough to learn them by heart and to associate them with a particular part of the service or season. When I learned that the name of the central prayer in the service, the Shema, meant "Listen," it made sense to me. All my life I had been receiving the tradition as ancient Israelites had: aurally.

This is probably why when I finally traveled to Israel, the language seemed so familiar. Had I stayed there a little while longer, I believe I would have begun to understand and speak it.

My father's newly-forged Friday ritual had a great effect on my life.

Eventually, the silver dollars he continued to save up for me were worth thousands. They paid for university, where I became a teacher and a writer. I still don't speak Hebrew or Yiddish, my ancestral *mamaloshen,* or regularly read the ancient texts, but from my father's gifts, I learned to pay attention to the words, to carve a line out of breath, to do everything with pure intention, so it becomes a kind of prayer.

Turn It and Turn It Again

Lisa Grunberger

Asking me about my Jewishness reminds me of that joke where an elder fish asks two younger fish, "How's the water today, boys?" The one younger fish says to the other: "What the hell is water?!" Being Jewish is so much a part of who I am, I can't define or separate it out. I think that's the point about Jewishness.

That I grew up with two Holocaust survivors and my Israeli born mother, that I'm married to a deeply spiritual Jewish man, that we send our daughter to a Jewish day school –– *this* is what comes closer to beginning to 'locate' my Jewishness. But they, too, do not fully get at it. These are the outer covering of my Jewishness, its garment. What is inside me, where my heart meets my *neshama*, well . . . I would have to recite Tehillim to you, or break into poetry, or just sit and watch the Shabbat candles dance in front of me. It's a sense and sensibility, a way of being; it's a prism through which I look at the world, the tilt of my Yiddishe *kopf* when I hear an ambulance.

I can offer anecdotes, small moments, woven in the weave of my Jewishness, mostly shaped by my mother Rachel's witty sensibility.

Rachel Broda Grunberger was born in British Mandate Palestine in 1925 and immigrated to the US in 1954. She met my father by the Mediterranean Sea in 1940 when he was walking along the shore, a homeless refugee from Berlin looking for his Tante Geeska, his mother's sister. My mother spoke German and invited him for dinner. The rest is history, a Jewish family history.

On my middle finger I wear the gold engagement ring my father gave to Mommy. It's engraved by Nachum, one of his "boat brothers," who arrived in Mandate Palestine in September 1939 on the illegal ship called the Noemi

Julia with my 19-year-old father. It says: "To Rachel Grunberger, August 13, 1943."

When I'm nervous, I turn it round and round. When I'm happy, I turn it round and round. Yes, they each died in my arms, six years apart, in their bed at home in Long Island, but they're always with me, guiding me, mooring me. Helping me laugh at life's absurdities.

§

"What if you find out you're not Jewish," my friend Christine asks me one afternoon when we're at the local playground with our children. I'd just told her I'd ordered a genealogy test to find my birth parents. She had forgotten I was adopted. "You just talk about your mom and dad so much and obviously loved them so much, I just, don't know…"

"…thought an adopted kid couldn't possibly have such a strong connection to her adopted parents?"

I don't mention the book I've been reading *Jews and Words* by Amos and Fania Oz. I've committed one sentence to memory: "Jewish continuity has always hinged on uttered and written words. … ours is not a bloodline but a text line." This tickles me. I just love how it stakes its claim and goes beyond blood fetish.

Christine's 'Jewish question' contains within it all the errors about adoption, inheritance, and Jewishness at once. It falsely assumes that to be Jewish runs through blood lines. You're not *really* Jewish unless it's biological. Just as Rachel and Robert Grunberger are not *really* my parents because they're not my biological parents. If I'd found out my birth parents are not Jewish, then what––my Jewishness is false? Like Barbra Streisand fearing: what will happen if I get a nose job and purchase a goyish nose, will I stop sounding like myself?

§

People tell me "You inherited your mother Rachel's gift for telling jokes and stories." I'm obsessed with transmitting stories about my parents to my daughter. I often tell her stories about my childhood, so she has a sense of her

Safta Rachel and Opa Robert.

Passover, circa 1982: Mom is sitting at the head of the table, all five foot one of her, a dynamo of a woman, a combination of Ruth Bader Ginsberg and Dr. Ruth Westheimer. She's telling one of her favorite jokes:

A Jewish man goes into the synagogue and prays. "O Lord, you know the mess I'm in, please let me win the lottery." The next week, he's back again. This time he's complaining. "O Lord, didn't you hear my prayer last week? I'll lose everything I hold dear unless I win the lottery." The third week, he comes back to the synagogue, and this time he's desperate. "O Lord, this is the third time I've prayed and pleaded to you to let me win the lottery—and still you don't help me!" Suddenly a booming voice sounds from heaven. "Benny, be reasonable. Meet me half way. Buy a lottery ticket!"

My mother's superpower was knowing how to live: Meet life half-way. Buy a lottery ticket. And ordinary life will happen, and during the course of an ordinary day, while you are at Macy's, say, inspecting the quality of a wool skirt by looking at its underside to see if it was double stitched, the ordinary takes on an extraordinary feeling. And thus, this extraordinary feeling of being with my mom at Macy's where she's looking at the underside of a wool skirt becomes a sacred place in my memory. Maybe this place is my sacred Jewish place. A place where one pays attention to the way things are made, a place where attention is paid.

My parents were profoundly Jewish in their devotion to tzedakah, to mitzvah, to kindness, to finding joy in the midst of loss, in their work ethic. My father probably never picked up a prayer book in his life, but he was the kindest man I've ever met. In how he cultivated his life, his generosity, he was a Hasid of the heart.

I was shaped by his gentle goodness; every time I pat my daughter's head, or stroke the calico, I can feel my father's gentle hand; the way he touched the world lives inside me. I choose to call this a Jewish hand that caresses Time, caresses Life.

§

I asked my Jewish husband about his Jewishness. In reply, he told me this joke:

Moshe's, a young Jewish man who had never been anywhere outside the town in which he was born, traveled from his small Polish shtetl to the great city of Warsaw. While he was away for several months, his friend Chaim impatiently waited for him to return and tell what he saw and experienced in the great city.

When Moshe finally returned, he told his friend Chaim of the wonders he'd seen.

"Chaim, my friend, you'll never believe it," he enthused. "In Warsaw, I met a Jew who owned a large factory with many employees. And I met a Jew who was a socialist and organized the unions against the factory and business owners. And I also met a Jew who was a Zionist and argued that all the Jews must unite, leave the exile, and move to Palestine. And I met a Jew who was deeply mystical, who said that trust in HaShem will provide for us wherever we are." With each meeting he recounted, Moshe's eyes grew wider with renewed amazement.

"So, Nu, Moshele," said Chaim, "What's so strange or surprising about all that? Warsaw's a big city. There must be at least a million Jews there."

"No, no, Chaimele, you don't understand! *It was the same Jew!*"

Me too. I'm the same Jew. I contain Jewish multitudes. Jewish character is not bound, it's fluid. What looks like a living contradiction or paradox remains mysterious. The final word will never be said. The professional definers of Jewishness can promulgate about what is a Jew, what isn't a Jew, but the lived, messy, spiritual, religious, social and cultural lives of Jews cannot be reduced to any doctrinal or halakhic definitions.

At my mother's funeral, I stood on the bima and told stories: "Mommy, you were not flesh of my flesh, but *neshama* of my *neshama*. Soul of my soul." When I'd ask Mom, do you believe in God, she'd say, "I believe in fate, but I'm not a fatalist." She was a Jew who loved a BLT, an Israeli who loved her adopted city of Manhattan, a mother who told me to "keep a part of yourself for yourself alone." I can still hear her belt out the Israeli National Anthem, the Hatikvah, off key, as she was terribly tone deaf. But her tikvah, her hope wasn't tone deaf at all; it was insistently joyful.

Life will pour over and beyond neat definitions. L'chaim! Through all versions of me, I am the same Jew who always recites the Shema before I fall asleep.

So, what of my Jewishness, Christine? What did the algorithmic tea leaves reveal about myself that I didn't already know deep in my Jewish neshama?

The poet and songwriter Leonard Cohen wrote: *Anyone who says / I'm not a Jew / is not a Jew/ I'm very sorry / but this decision / is final.*

Let Cohen's response be my own.

What We Carry: Rituals, Judaica Passing It All Down

What We Carry
Dina Elenbogen

My grandfather Saul, imprisoned in Russia for socialist activities in the early 1900's, carried my Grandma Ida's Passover dishes from the basement, up the narrow steps of their tiny Chicago apartment. My grandmother kept a strictly kosher home. Saul, ten years her senior, believed that religion only separated people from each other. He carried them anyway, a labor that expressed his love for his wife.

Until she was fifteen, Ida lived in a Russian shtetl, a world of poverty and shared rituals. In America, to feel a sense of belonging, Ida made kosher meals from scratch and separated her dishes between dairy and meat. On Passover her kitchen was as kosher as those of her Orthodox neighbors. Her china was made in occupied Japan during World War II, the war Ida's three sons had fought in. She acquired those dishes when her four children were already grown. The ones that Saul carried must have been the cheap ones from Woolworths, some of which also made their way to my parents' cupboard and then to the cupboards of my home.

Ida's youngest son, my father Gil, has lived a century, now in a condo outside of Chicago. His biggest ailment is his hearing, destroyed when he was a flight engineer who dropped bombs on Nazi Germany. When his memory begins to fail more, and when he dies, he will take with him these remnants of history.

Rabbi Jonathan Sacks believes we pass on history through story, so this fragment of story, this act of koshering the kitchen so strictly on Passover, is the history Ida passed on to my father that he later passed on to me. Maybe we pass down history not only through what we carry, but *how* we carry. Do we carry dishes, rituals, laws and ethics as burdens, or is our carrying more like a dance or a song, a gift of belonging to something larger than ourselves?

In the shtetl, was *kashrut* the quiet, even subversive, way that Jews expressed their identity under persecution? Was there no place for joy? Ida's father was a cantor, so there was once song and prayer. He was also a *schochet,* a ritual slaughterer, who slit an animal's throat according to Jewish law, to lessen its suffering.

Ida didn't bring to America her father's way of praying. She sang Russian songs with her sisters, spoke Yiddish to keep secrets, but she never learned to pray in Hebrew. I imagine she never felt like she fully belonged to any language or country.

Seated in the green chair in the corner of my father's large sunny apartment, I try to substantiate my imaginings of the past, to make sure I am carrying what my ancestors had meant to pass on or if something got lost in translation.

My father agrees that keeping a kosher kitchen was how his mother expressed her Judaism. "That's what she thought Jews did, so she did it as well." His answer reminds me that Ida didn't come from a generation like mine that has the luxury to contemplate how we want to express our Jewish identities. It was easy enough for her to own two cheap sets of dishes (before she later got the china), and there were several kosher butcher shops in their Chicago neighborhoods, my father explains.

I ask if, besides the kosher food and dishes, there was singing at the Sabbath table. He shakes his head, sadly, there were no songs but perhaps occasionally a prayer for wine.

My father is the only one of his siblings who brought anything Jewish into their home once they married. His sister wanted to get away from what made her stand out from others in her milieu. My father, who felt a sense of belonging mostly in Jewish communities, also acknowledges that because he stayed home the longest and ran the kitchen when his father fell ill, the burden (or gift) landed on his shoulders. Wherever they lived, even after my parents married, my grandmother would continue hosting Jewish holidays and Shabbat dinner. Toward the end of my grandfather Saul's life, he began to believe in the value of Judaism. When my father was 73, a widower, he became a Bar Mitzvah.

I've carried boxes of kosher Passover dishes up the steps of my college and young adult apartment, and now, up the steps of the home I share with my family. I've scrubbed my counters until they sparkled like Ida's kitchen. While carrying my traditions, I've also found joy: in the communities of like-minded Jews I met in college and graduate school and the kosher Shabbat dinners we shared and in the literary and social action communities I've belonged to. I discovered this joyful belonging most profoundly during the year I spent in Israel. There was the awe I felt as the peace of Shabbat descended on Jerusalem. The warmth I experienced hearing Shalom Aleichem, the prayer calling the angels to visit for Sabbath, as it floated through the open windows from one home to the next in the northern town of Ma'alot. The exuberance I shared with the men in the apartment below mine, as they banged their fists on the table and sang out prayers on Shabbat morning. My understanding of the diversity of Jews also expanded as I sat at my Sephardic neighbors' Passover table and did the sacred work of welcoming home to Israel, Jews from Ethiopia.

There were cantors on both sides of my family in my great grandparents' generation, so once, there must have been celebratory singing— even if the songs didn't make it to American tables. And maybe sometimes they did. My parents' wedding at the Blackstone Hotel in Chicago was described by family and friends as one of the most freilach (joyful) events they'd ever attended. My father attributes this to his Labor Zionist friends he found in his early twenties and their wild Israeli dancing and singing.

Those same friends would later invite us to their Passover seders where the food and dishes weren't kosher, but the room was filled with spirit, song, and tradition.

Our children's matzoh covers and our homemade *haggadot* grace our seders even now that the kids are grown. My daughter, who is studying to be a cantor, has always brought music to every square foot of our home.

When I think of how the hard work of cleaning for Passover and carrying our second-rate dishes sapped my energy to the point where I had no time left to plan the perfect seder, I imagine being handed Ida's tattered box of dishes, a ragged sponge with which to sterilize counters and corners and shelves. While these tasks gave me a sense of belonging and continuity, sometimes they also became my Egypt.

Last Pesach, we washed our rest-of-the-year china twice in the dishwasher to purify it. Instead of carrying dishes from the basement, we carried my father up the porch steps to our table. He saw how the traditions his mother once carried on the boat or up the steps to her first apartment, landed on our table, differently, still creating a Jewish home.

The dishes gleamed and daffodils from our garden filled vases. Most importantly, we told the story of our Exodus. My daughter taught us a new song that our voices carried to the tune of remembering. And sometimes to the tune of letting go.

Papa's *Tallit*

Sandell Morse

Papa, my grandfather, stands in front the bathroom sink as if it were an altar. He winds *teffilin,* phylacteries, around his forearm, hand, and head. On each of the two leather straps, a small box. Inside each box, verses from Exodus and Deuteronomy. Papa centers one box on his biceps, the other on his forehead. He is binding his heart and his mind to God. I am eleven, and I have been watching Papa wind *teffilin* ever since I learned to toddle. He kisses each end of the collar of his *tallit,* lifts the prayer shawl high, and brings it to rest on his head as if it were a hood. He drapes an end over each arm. Now, he prays, *Baruch atah Adonai eloheinu ....* I chant along inside my head, and the music of centuries moves inside my body. Papa bows over and over, as Orthodox men do, as if they are saying yes to what is holy. I have no idea what Papa is saying, and that's a good thing, because every morning when he prays, Papa thanks God that he was not born a woman. I also have no idea we are breaking a commandment that forbids worship in a toilet.

The mirror over the sink reflects our faces, my blue-green eyes and curly light brown hair, Papa's soft brown eyes and gray comb over. The pungent scent of apple tobacco escapes from the pouch in Papa's pocket. In the kitchen, water runs in the sink. My mother is filling the percolator. Upstairs, my father sleeps. In the bedroom Papa shares with Mama, I imagine Mama sitting at her dressing table and applying cold cream to her cheeks.

I love standing beside Papa these early mornings. Prayer, it seems, clears the air of my father's derision and distain. He is a Reform Jew. No Mumbo Jumbo for him. Mumbo Jumbo is code for Hebrew. Mumbo Jumbo is also racist, but I don't know that yet.

My friend Carol is studying for her Bat Mitzvah and learning Hebrew. I want a Bat Mitzvah, too. "No," my father says. "You're Reformed."

None of us says Reform, which is correct.

"Please," I say.

"You heard me," my father says.

§

I follow my father's path to assimilation. I am an on again, off again Jew. As a family, my husband, my three sons, and I light Hanukkah candles and invite guests to our Passover Seder. Once in a while, I attend services at a synagogue. None of our sons becomes a Bar Mitzvah. Yet, somehow my family absorbs the spirit of Judaism that Papa passed on to me.

I am shopping for a *tallit*. At sixteen, Raina, my granddaughter, will become a Bat Mitzvah in Denver, Colorado. At thirteen, she memorized her Torah portion, but she could not tell anyone what the words meant. Meaning is essential to Jewish learning. In becoming a Bat Mitzvah, Raina is asking to join a community that has argued with and interpreted this text for centuries. Her class celebrated their Bat and Bar Mitzvahs without her. Determined, Raina continued her studies with Cantor Regina Heit, a woman who tucked Raina under her wing. A cantor sings the prayers, and I imagine that Cantor Heit and Raina connected through music. Raina is a clear soprano; she loves to sing. She's eager and enthusiastic.

Inside Kolbo, a Judaica store in Brookline, Massachusetts, *tallitot* are arranged according to fabric. I finger pure silk and remember the rough wool of Papa's *tallit* and the *tzitzit*, braided strings hanging down. Raina will wear an ivory lace dress. I hold up a cobalt blue *tallit* with a hand-painted scene of the heavenly city of Jerusalem along one border. She will love this. On the plane from Logan Airport in Boston to DIA, I open my oversized purse again and again. *Yes, the tallit is here.*

In a room adjacent to the sanctuary inside Temple Emmanuel, Cantor Heit wraps my granddaughter in her cobalt blue silk *tallit*. Raina traces the outline of a golden dome and says, "Grammy, it's unbelievably beautiful."

She is unbelievably beautiful.

Cantor Heit recites the blessing for donning a *tallit*, first in Hebrew, then in English. I latch on to three words: time, space, and holiness. I feel them all, the time of generations, the space of mystery, and the holiness of this moment.

§

Three weeks after Raina's Bat Mitzvah, the family gathers at our home on the coast of Maine, and I become a Bat Mitzvah, too. I am seventy-four. I have been studying with my dear friend, Rabbi Lev. I don't learn Hebrew. Not a requirement, according to Lev. Besides, he says, I won't like a lot of what the prayers are saying, anyway. I think of Papa.

In preparation for my Bat Mitzvah, each of my grandchildren and I choose a book we will read together. The books are age appropriate with themes exploring family dynamics, responsibility, moral clarity, and activism. Each child completes a project, a poster, an exchange of emails, a drawing. To learn about my father's family, Nina and I cook. For years, my mother had searched cookbooks for a recipe my father remembered from his childhood — his mother's velvet pudding. "Ambrosia," he would say. A generation later, the internet yielded. In the kitchen, Nina separated eggs, and as I beat the whites, I told her stories about my dad and his Proustian velvet pudding. We pronounced the pudding good, but not the ambrosia of memory.

The Saturday evening of my Bat Mitzvah, I read my Torah portion in English. My commentary is from a short story I wrote that turned the tale of Adam and Eve into a feminist *midrash*. My protagonist, Bessie, a Jewish grandmother, is dismayed that her son, who lives in California, is raising his two girls as Catholics. One day when Bessie visits, she tells her youngest granddaughter the story of Adam and Eve from a Jewish feminist point view. Bessie says, "That Eve was some smart cookie. She bit the apple and brought us all into a world of knowledge."

The theme of my life and my Bat Mitzvah.

The ceremony begins. Raina wraps me in my *tallit*, and I feel the textures of generations. The *tallit* is God's warm embrace; it is the community's warm embrace; it is Raina's warm embrace.

My three sons are here, one divorced, two with their wives along with my three granddaughters and my grandson. Friends and family are here. I have chosen to close my Bat Mitzvah with the *Havdalah* service that ends *Shabbat*. That afternoon, my grandchildren and I filled small mesh bags with spices: whole cloves, whole nutmeg, and cinnamon sticks. Zeke, my grandson, hauls back and tosses each bag into the crowd, and this small rebellion brings a smile to my lips. He is ten, and all weekend, he has been trying to find his place among my three vibrant granddaughters, all older and more outgoing than he. I hold a spice bag to my nose and breathe *Shabbat's* sweetness along with the scents of cloves, cinnamon, and nutmeg. I breathe the aroma of Papa's pungent apple tobacco. I see our faces in the bathroom mirror, Papa's brown eyes, his gray comb over, my blue-green eyes and curls. I am a daughter of the Covenant, and I want to tell Papa, but I think he knows.

Inheritance

Joan Leegant

I was constantly misplacing the candlesticks. Every time I'd clean out the wooden sideboard stuffed with things I never used but couldn't throw away—a hand-painted soup terrine my mother had insisted was rare French porcelain (eventually determined to be, yes, French, no, not rare), the tarnished silver tea service salvaged from my in-laws' estate, the cut glass candy dish that has never held candy—I'd take out the two candlesticks, study them, consider what to do with them, then put them somewhere a notch above the never-to-use sideboard and below the actually functional. They were bent to the point of alarming, a jagged edge at the midpoints where the parts had been poorly soldered together and where you could slice a finger if you weren't careful. They were also discolored, a faded brass blackened at the edges and the base, which had always looked like a mismatch, another bad soldering job.

But I held onto them because they had belonged to my grandmother and my grandmother was the one member of our family connected to Jewish ritual. An immigrant from Minsk who lived her American life in the Bronx, her six children—in that now familiar American story—had abandoned Jewish practice as soon as possible, jettisoning not only the Friday night candle-lighting but the kosher food and most of the holidays and, eventually, the Bronx itself. They fanned out to Long Island and Queens and upstate New York; the unmarried daughter moved to Manhattan. There was no grandfather in the picture; my mother's father existed only in name and family lore, most of it unreliable. Some said he abandoned her. Others claimed that it was she who did the rending, refusing to follow him to Chicago or some other more exotic locale to pursue a business opportunity beyond the outer limits of the five boroughs.

How I came to know that she was the keeper of the literal Jewish flame, I don't know. My parents left the Bronx in the great post-war migration to the suburbs when I was five, and I have no memories of being in my grandmother's apartment over shabbat before that; if I had, I wouldn't have known what it was. It's likely that she observed the shabbat alone, not in the sense of loneliness but of privacy. It mattered to her, if to no one else in her orbit, so she lit the candles and said the blessing. She was a principled woman, often stoic, not especially warm nor needy, which I liked. She was the opposite of my mother, whose neediness could overwhelm. Was there a ritual challah? Possibly, but if her children ever learned the words of the motzi, I never heard any of them say it. In my imagining, I see my grandmother murmuring the bracha, or perhaps saying it silently, and distributing the bread, not expecting the children to learn it from her.

I do, however, have a photograph of my grandmother standing over her shabbat candles. She's wearing an apron, and the candles stand on a small table in the hall. Who took it? Again, I don't know. I also don't remember receiving the candlesticks. Most likely it was my mother who gave them to me, knowing, however unhappily, of my interest in Jewish ritual. This would have been when I was in my early thirties and newly returned from three years in Israel, some of it spent at a modern yeshiva. By then, my grandmother had been dead ten years and nobody else would have wanted them. To my mother, my desire to take on Jewish observance was hurtful, even a betrayal; she believed it was a form of judgment, though I knew it was simple guilt: she'd abandoned it all, to her own mother's thinly veiled disgust, and now here came this daughter, resurrecting all that old-fashioned hocus-pocus and becoming my grandmother's proxy, as if to say: *You didn't think you'd get away with it without feeling bad, did you?*

I cherished the candlesticks when I first received them and thought that surely they were valuable. I wondered if my grandmother had brought them with her on the boat from Russia when she was fourteen, crossing the ocean with her two sisters, fifteen and sixteen, the candlesticks hidden in the folds of a coat or buried in a suitcase of bed linens, an heirloom going back generations. I conjured a line of pious matriarchs stretching back centuries, keepers of the flame despite—or maybe because of—undependable husbands and ungrateful children. I pictured a series of women's faces, all the same, passing the items one to the other like in a touching story by a more sentimental version of Sholom Aleichem. I've since learned that in fact they are an inexpensive brass set commonly sold on the Lower East Side to poor immigrants like my grandmother, knockoffs of a high-quality brand manufactured in the late 19th century by a company in Warsaw.

Although I've had my grandmother's candlesticks for forty years, I've never used them. By the time my mother gave them to me, I'd acquired a three-candle candelabra made of green enamel and brass with *Shabbat Shalom* engraved in Hebrew on the base, one of my first purchases in Jerusalem after I'd taken on the observant lifestyle I would later let go of. I bought another pair ten years into my marriage, a sleek silver set I polished each week to a high sheen with my young sons. More recently, while teaching at a university in Oklahoma, I found a short square crystal set in a vintage shop, perfectly sized for the standard three-hour white candles that, together, give the whole operation a pearly glow. Other sets have arrived over the years, some as gifts—from an Israeli friend who stayed with us, from a thankful student—others whose provenance I no longer recall. Because there is no shortage of candlesticks in our house, I tell myself there is no need to line up my grandmother's blackened half-broken pair alongside the others. They are not aesthetically pleasing, they wouldn't align with the rest, they're hazardous.

But that's not the truth. The truth is that my grandmother's candlesticks are a carrier of sadness, even pain. I cannot see them, and my grandmother, without seeing my mother. Did my grandmother love my mother? It's the wrong question. My grandmother did what women with limited emotional stores do with six children: feed, clothe and tend to all, dote, if they're lucky, on a few. Did my mother love me? Again, the wrong question. And the same answer. My mother did not like my inverse rebellion, taking it as a stab in the heart, just as my grandmother didn't like my mother's more explicit one. And I, flapping in the wind between the two of them, could safely land nowhere.

I wish I could say that my grandmother's candlesticks were the treasured repository of my family's Jewishness, handed down from generation to generation even if they skipped one. I wish I could assign them the nostalgia and sentimental value they would seem, with their Lower East Side knockoff origins and hundred-year provenance, to demand. I wish I could turn them into the sweet heirlooms I envy in other people's living rooms--the sepia photographs, the pocket watch someone's father got for his bar mitzvah, the taped together ketubah signed by a rabbi in the Old Country preserved in a glass frame.

But I can't. Alongside the beloved candelabra acquired during my life-changing years in Jerusalem and the stately silver columns I lovingly polished with my sons, these candlesticks, with their sadness and disappointment soldered on as clumsily as their bases, are also mine.

And so I keep them, somewhere. I can't always find them, and seldom, nowadays, look for them, but I know they aren't gone.

A Sage Gift

Julie Zuckerman

Bookmarks are found in every corner of my house in central Israel, wedged between pages, inside night tables and kitchen drawers, under piles of bills and mail, on the shelves that used to house my kids' toys and games and old Purim costumes but are now crammed with books. I appreciate them all, but only one is exquisite: a bookmark given as a wedding party favor, hand-painted and calligraphed by my friend Elly, mother of the groom.

Wavy tones of emerald and fern green serve as the bookmark's border, where the thick paper has absorbed varying degrees of the watercolors. In the center, a stalk of מרווה דגולה *marva degula*, salvia viridis, common sage, a grand purple flower at the top and new buds forming along the stem. On the back, Elly has written a detailed explanation of why she chose sage. She quotes from the Song of Songs, one of the five sacred scrolls, in which an allegory of lovers symbolizes the relationship between God and people. We read it on Passover, which begins a few days after the wedding.

דּוֹדִי צַח וְאָדוֹם דָּגוּל מֵרְבָבָה

My beloved is clear-skinned and ruddy, Preeminent among ten thousand.

Her mini-drash explains that she's chosen the pasuk for the similarity in the words *dagul mervava* with *marva degula*: "'dagul mervava' is "very highly valued, very fine, revered," a definition fitting the "union of a couple that we appreciate and admire and we are so happy they have found each other."

Wild sage is in bloom all over Israel in April, including in my backyard. I snap a picture of the bookmark next to my sage and send it to her. A perfect replica.

We share many interests, Elly and I, though we are not close. I marvel at the hours she put into this bookmark project. She made at least 150. She is not an artist by trade, but a speech therapist turned early reading teacher. All four of my children learned to read English in her classes. Today, she is tour guide at Neot Kedumim, the nature reserve down the road, where one can find every plant and tree mentioned in the bible, along with scientific explanations and commentaries from our own sages, the great thinkers and rabbis and writers in Jewish history. Elly started painting the plants as a pandemic project, when tourism ground to a halt, the reserve was closed, and she was furloughed. Fortunately, the reserve is open again.

Perhaps I ought to frame the bookmark, or a series of them, but this seems antithetical to their raison d'etre. I imagine they'd be bereft to be forcibly retired. They are placeholders, dividers between past and future, transitions. Elly's bookmark has a ribbon on top that peeks out from the pages, an invitation to dive back into the solace and contentment derived from reading.

I do not luxuriate over silks or fine jewels, expensive perfumes or Italian wines. My primary indulgence—the only gift I ever want—is books. Of course, Elly did not hand-paint the bookmark for me alone, but I treasure the gift for all it represents: a love of reading, Jewish texts and wisdom. A pause that calls us to begin again. Wonder in the natural world, our ties to the land of Israel. The celebration of two souls creating a union, something—love—from nothing. Gratitude for our people, our books, our land, our traditions, and all we hold dear.

When the Moon Calls Us

Mimi Zieman

It's always been Passover that I enjoyed most, maybe because it's the first time I stealthily drank wine, as I dipped egg matzahs in Manischewitz before drenching them in melted chocolate for our family's famed (in our eyes!) matzah layer cake. After each dip, I swigged a thimble-full of wine.

"She's tipsy," Mom guffawed to my grandmother as I made loopy noises from the kitchen table while licking my fingers.

During the Seder, I loved how the horseradish "cleared our sinuses" and how my friend's father made the same dad joke every year. His eyes got wide, and his Snidely Whiplash mustache seemed to touch the walls.

"Why do we eat hard-boiled eggs in salt water?" he asked.

"Because when the Jews crossed the Red Sea escaping Egypt, the water came up to their balls!" (The word for eggs in Hebrew is the same word as for testicles.)

The repetition of rituals made this holiday a clear standout. I'd always attended Jewish schools, so I relished creating Haggadahs, drawing images of the four sons, and stapling the corners of construction paper to fashion colorful plates for holding matzahs. It helps that the Seder is democratic; we go around the table taking turns reading. Everyone has a voice, and it's the only time all year I practice reading Hebrew out loud.

My father was Latvian, the sole survivor of his family from the Holocaust, and fifteen years older than my mother, who was born in Israel, then called Palestine. My parents met in Germany after the war, immigrated to New York City by ship, and soon discovered they were horribly mismatched. My mother had strong opinions and was as tough as they came. My father wanted to live life as he pleased, girlfriends and all. Just one of the many emotional consequences of surviving his time as a slave laborer in Siberia (and so many other things).

My bedroom shared a wall with theirs, and rage seeped through. I got used to shrinking, hiding, keeping my thoughts and words to myself. My gut got used to feeling tight and leaden. Dad moved out when I was around seven. Divorce followed.

Their arguing continued, mostly on the phone and mostly about bills. But while I was in high school, Mom started inviting Dad to the Seders. She let him lead them. Since Dad's dream was to perform Yiddish theater, he took any opportunity to sing as loudly as possible, his voice rising above everyone else's in the room. He conducted the Seder like a maestro, commanded the space like a diva.

I attended college in Montreal, and during Freshman year I was only supposed to come home for winter break. But on a cold day in March, my first love broke up with me unexpectedly. I needed my family. I needed Passover. So, I boarded a train for a twelve-hour ride to New York City and surprised them on the eve of the holiday. The swelling harmonies of Ma Nishtana and Dayenu soothed me like a salve.

The only sad thing about this memory is what happened to the Tupperwares full of matzah ball soup and gefilte fish I brought back with me to school. When this man of heartbreak visited my dorm room to check up on me, I reached into my mini fridge and handed over my treasures. I wish I could take back that moment, along with the taste of home.

At twenty-two, I slung on a backpack to hike around Nepal. This didn't quite mesh with my background—I was raised in an Orthodox community in New York. My mother characterized this trip with her favorite word: Ridiculous! But even she was no match for the strong pull I felt in my gut to go to the Himalayas. I hesitate to use the word "calling," but what else would overtake all reason?

The etymology of the word calling is "outcry, shouting," and also "a summons or invitation." Here, my leadened gut and my shrunken self summoned me away from the shouting in our house, the clamor of our city, the thunder of shattered expectations.

On the third day of my solo trek, I spread out my sleeping bag beside a waterfall, under a starry sky. Seeing the full circle of the shining moon, I realized it was Passover. The Haggadah says, "in every generation, each person is obligated to see themselves as if they personally came forth from Egypt." They should imagine themselves experiencing liberation from slavery firsthand. That night, I connected with my ancestors as a wanderer. That night, freedom meant everything was possible and nothing was predictable. That night, I was freed from any box in which I had lived. Daughter. Student. Good girl. Quiet girl. I was freed from every voice telling me what to do, there was no *You'll do as I say young lady* and *This is my house, I say what goes*.

I lay in my sleeping bag, listening only to the branches creak and the water tumble. I would soon learn to hear my own voice, beckoned by the echo of Passover, words pinging through my cells, veins of memories, harmonies of throat, lamenting oppression, celebrating freedom, reclining, imbibing, inviting the stranger.

Our holidays are marked by the moon, the tides of the sea and the phases of the sky threading through us like the blue yarns of a tallit. Our tradition, so rich, summons us to glance upwards to be guided. To inhale the light, reflect it, exhale the darkness. To awaken us to the subtleties in between, waxing, waning, crescent, gibbous, where the light sometimes hides.

Several years later, I was back in the Himalayas, this time on a formal Everest expedition in Tibet. In this wilderness, we'd seen no other westerners for weeks while severe snowstorms pummeled us and delayed our hike to Base Camp. When we finally arrived, my body drenched in snow, my mind disordered by high altitude, we started the grueling task of pitching tents and repacking goods for our trek to Advanced Base Camp, close to 18,000 feet elevation.

The night before leaving, it was déjà vu with the moon. Totally unaware of the date, I knew it was Passover. This time, I had access to a tent, food, and the company of five teammates (none of them Jewish) whom I could invite to a Seder.

I scrounged through our barrels of food and cooked hard-boiled eggs, made charoset, and used sea toast crackers for matzah. I lit candles and called on twenty-five years of repetition to share my ancestral journey with these elite adventurers.

As we leaned into the table, the elbows of our down jackets touching, I asked, "How is this night different from all others?" I felt seen for the first time since our expedition had started.

After the Seder, I rummaged through my duffle for stationery to write my mother a letter about how I'd lit yontif candles in the wilderness. It would be carried by local mail runners taking close to a week to reach the valley to post. I thought about her and my grandmother cooking until the wee hours, gefilte fish steaming in the pot, liver and onions sizzling on the stove.

Nineteen years later, I visited New York City from our home in Atlanta with my husband and three children for Passover. My father had been diagnosed with pancreatic cancer ten months earlier. He was gaunt and weak but still himself when we arrived on a Friday morning, the first Seder scheduled for Monday. But he didn't make it. He died early Monday when it was still dark, the full moon shining somewhere.

That night, we gathered at Mom's Seder table along with my brother and his children and my father's current wife. We tucked napkins into our collars to cover our chests, mimicking the way my father did. We sang at the top of our lungs, mimicking the way my father did. We laughed as hard as we cried. We connected with him through the echo of his words in the walls, our voices rising together, a calling that briefly freed us from grief.

Christmas Dinner Miami Style:
A Hanukkah Fish Tale

Amy Rogers

If it's Christmas and you're Jewish, that usually means one thing: Chinese food for dinner.

And that's exactly what my siblings and I had planned. My sister Julie and I would get sesame chicken takeout in Tallahassee, and our brother Adam would get spicy beef delivered to his high-rise condo in Miami. We do a version of this every year, separately in our two cities.

Like lots of families, we visit infrequently. We mean to do better, but time has a way of rushing by. Our cities are 500 miles apart, a dicey drive across the Sunshine State, even when it's not the height of holiday travel. So never, ever do we get together at Christmas.

But 2024 was different. I thought back over the previous year. Our Aunt Lynne was widowed when our beloved family patriarch, Uncle Bill, passed away. My sister's partner, Elgin, had died as well. My brother, a heart transplant recipient, hadn't been feeling great. Suddenly, I realized it had been almost a year since we sisters had seen our youngest sibling. And that was entirely too long.

Now, roughly three times in 100 years, the first night of Hanukkah falls on December 25. It was happening this year. "If we took turns driving and brought lots of snacks, the drive wouldn't be so terrible," I suggested to my sister.

"We can listen to podcasts and take breaks along the way," she agreed.

Lynne invited us to dinner at her lovely condo in the tower next door to my brother. I pictured us sitting down to a real holiday meal, with Lynne's succulent brisket or mustard-glazed lamb and creamy potatoes to soak up the juices. We'd celebrate together as a family, instead of noshing on takeout in separate cities.

Julie and I started packing.

As if zig-zagging 1,000 miles across Florida at Christmastime isn't nutty enough, I also unintentionally set in motion a raft of culinary complications.

I'd seen a funny post online in "We Love Jewish Food," a Facebook group with more than 128,000 members. Les Degen, a stand-up comedian based on Long Island, posted:

"Being that Hanukkah falls on the same day as Christmas this year, my family will be celebrating the Feast of the Seven Fishes with white fish, gefilte fish, kippered salmon, pickled herring, sable, sturgeon, and lox."

Unless you're Italian or you live in a city with a lot of people who are, you might not know about the tradition of serving a lavish Christmas meal comprised of seven or more kinds of fish. Many of these—lobster, clams, and other shellfish—are *trayf*. Observant Jews don't eat them.

I texted the post to my siblings on December 19. The "ha-ha" emoji came back.

Degen's quip is my favorite kind of humor. It's observational, timely, and clever. But I could never have expected what happened next.

Just a couple of days before the trip, my brother called. "They don't have sable at Costco. Lynne has the sturgeon, lox, whitefish salad, and seafood salad."

"Wait, what?"

"I need to get the sable from the deli," he explained.

I was incredulous. "You're actually doing it?"

"Of course," he replied, as if there'd never been any doubt. He's a master of understatement.

My aunt and my brother had taken the offhand joke I sent and, without telling me, made it into *the actual menu* for our family dinner on December 25, the first night of Hanukkah.

I burst out laughing. A few moments later I noticed my eyes were watering and I had a lump in my throat.

I called Lynne.

"Thank you for doing this," I said.

"I'm making latkes, too."

That lump in my throat didn't subside until a couple hours later.

Hanukkah, many Jews will say, isn't a major holiday. It's not commanded that we observe it. In the U.S., it's morphed into an awkward Christmas-adjacent amalgam of historical remembrance and modern-day gift-giving.

But as a child, I always loved the Hanukkah story. I could picture the scrappy Maccabees, a rag-tag band of soldiers rushing in to reclaim the Temple that invaders had defiled. I imagined the Maccabees discovering the precious vessel of oil to light their way as they worked, the slightest amount of oil miraculously lasting the entire eight days it took to clean and rededicate the Temple. And yes, I loved the presents. What child wouldn't?

And so, Julie and I made our way down I-10, the Florida Turnpike, and finally I-95 toward Miami.

My contribution to the dinner would be homemade *gelt* I made by pouring melted chocolate into little silicone molds of coins with stars of David and menorahs. But as delighted as I was, the *kvetch* in me had noticed a small but looming problem with our dinner plan.

We had just five fish dishes represented in a feast of seven. Only the pettiest of people would mention such a thing. Just thinking it was ridiculous! Nonetheless, I didn't want to fall short on a challenge I myself had issued, due to a technicality. I'd sneakily planned a workaround just in case.

At sundown on December 25, we said the *barucha* and lit the candle for the first night of Hanukkah. Lynne placed the platters of luscious fish and crispy latkes on the glass-topped serving buffet. Her daughter, two grandsons, and a girlfriend joined us as we all filled our plates. From the tote bag I'd packed back home, I pulled out two small tins and placed them on the buffet: one of sardines and one of smoked oysters. That made seven fishes, total. No one could say the Rogers family failed to understand the assignment.

Although the oysters aren't allowed for us Jews, in this instance, they did their job simply by showing up. Whether we're counting eight nights of light, seven fishes to feast upon, or two sisters and a brother who finally made time for each other, it was the most memorable family meal we'd shared in years. Now, about Passover coming up: Let's discuss.

Hachnasat Orchim

Talya Jankovits

Hospitality is a mitzvah tracing back to one of the first Jewish forefathers, Abraham. A unique feature of Abraham's tent was its openings on all four sides. This was so that a traveler passing his home, from any angle, would not miss an opportunity for much needed food, shelter, or rest. Abraham was the first Jewish host with the most. His eagerness to welcome passersby into his home became the foundation of the Jewish value of hosting guests. So much so is this mentality embedded in the Jewish culture that it is even written into the Passover Haggadah: "Let all who are hard-pressed come and eat. Let all who are in need come and share the Passover sacrifice." This was also a mantra of the third-century Babylonian sage Rav Huna, who was known to make this statement when he sat down to every meal: "Let all who are in need come and eat!" And this was a value and lifestyle approach my parents embodied in its most sincere form.

Living in the Orthodox Jewish community of Los Angeles in the 80's to early 2000's, our family found itself in the heart of a neighborhood steadily expanding. It attracted observant newcomers seeking a reprieve from harsh East Coast winters, immigrants who landed in the city of angels, and a large number of local secular Jews curious about the observant lifestyle. A Jewish outreach program called The Jewish Learning Exchange (JLE), founded in 1980, was created to link all these individuals with hospitable community members. Somehow, a staff member at JLE connected with my parents and asked them if they would be willing to host various families and singles who needed meals for Shabbat or the chagim. My mother, a *ba'al teshuva* who became observant of Orthodox Judaism at the age of nineteen, and my father, a frum-from-birth Jew from southern Memphis and a child of Holocaust survivors, were more than happy to oblige. Many times in their single lives, they found themselves the recipients of this same kind of hospitality that was being asked of them. They felt a personal investment in a value that fostered their own relationships with Judaism.

As a *ba'al teshuva*, my artist mother was excited to connect with people like herself who grew up secular and were drawn to the beauty of Orthodox Judaism, and my father, a psychologist who grew up in a small-town Jewish community, found the idea of growth and connectivity attractive. They remained the perfect duo for the task. Their combined religious and educational backgrounds provided a balanced approach to outreach, and their natural divide of domestic tasks resulted in wholesome and inspiring Shabbat experiences that left guests always asking to return. One big draw for our returning guests was my mother's cooking.

My mother was a whiz in the kitchen. Her food was atypical for a Jewish housewife of the 80's. Despite her full-time job as an occupational therapist and raising five kids, her creative instincts made her ripe for churning out delectable dishes each week, favorites like Moroccan fish, Tajin chicken, moussaka, and skordalia, which graced our tables and delighted our guests. My father, sociable and outgoing, was always cracking jokes whilst also providing profound insights and explanations of the various customs, keeping visitors both laughing and reflective. His very traditional dress of a black suit, white shirt, and a black hat, and my mother's bohemian style of loose dresses and flowing skirts along with her turban-wrapped hair, charmed guests from all walks of life. They felt they found a perfect marriage of tradition and authenticity, a ying to a yang – the true embodiment of my unlikely paired parents. These guests felt they found a place welcoming to all, and it was, perhaps the precise reason JLE recruited my parents.

The JLE program was founded on good intentions which were often met with poor execution. This was long before the time of cell phones when broken-telephone was an actual real-life problem and not just a schoolyard game. Phone calls were made mid to late week with vague references of who would be joining us for a Shabbat dinner or lunch. Often guests were only given my parents' name and address, and my parents were only given a number of guests to expect with little context. This faulty system resulted in uncomfortable and humorous situations. While my parents may have expected a young couple for a Friday night dinner, a large family might have shown up instead—for Shabbat lunch! Guests who spoke only a few words of English might have mistakenly arrived an hour early for a Friday night dinner, forcing my mother to break her tongue trying to keep them entertained as we awaited my father to finally return from shul. Or perhaps, no guests showed up at all and we all ate timidly, wondering if somewhere in the neighborhood our guests wandered looking for our home, or perhaps they mistakenly showed up to other unassuming hosts.

We became pros at anticipating the unanticipated. Like an expert team of master non-verbal communicators, we solved each hosting challenge as it arose. We kids would read the high-pitched notes of our mother receiving guests at the door and do quick headcounts, assessing how many extra place settings needed to be added to the table while my mother stalled at the door. My parents never wanted a guest to feel uncomfortable, so this quick fix was always done discreetly. After too many snafus, my parents devised a new plan. They got into the habit of setting an extra place at the table regardless of whether they committed to hosting guests or not. It became standard and natural that when setting our table, we automatically added an extra seat. This became our family tradition.

Whenever neighbors, both Orthodox and not, dropped by right before or during one of our meals, they could count on a seat waiting for them, as if their arrival was always anticipated. Regardless of their insistence that they weren't hungry, or already ate, they would eventually fill those plates with my mother's cooking. Though often that seat might have remained unfilled, its significance was not lost on me and my siblings. It was the physical manifestation of my parents' kindness, their thoughtfulness, their consideration.

Over the many years that my parents participated in the JLE program, they, like Abraham, were the 'hosts with the most'. They made lifelong friends and lasting impressions on others. One Russian family who had recently immigrated experienced their first seder in my parents' home. Ever the considerate hosts, my parents bought Russian Haggadahs especially for them—the first they ever read through. To this day, my mother recalls that particular meal and the translation game they played. My father translated my mother's English into Yiddish, and the visiting mother translated the Yiddish into Russian. Punchlines to jokes arrived several minutes late, but that particular evening transcended the differences of diasporic Jews and brought us together into a single meal of connectivity.

My parents were honored to offer many people their very first Shabbat or Yom Tov meal through the JLE. Guests always embraced the experience with love and enthusiasm. We met many interesting and entertaining people through this program, and though, eventually, my parents teetered out of the program, one thing stayed: the extra place setting at the table.

To this day, my parents, now in their seventies and living in an apartment in Jerusalem, still set an extra place at their table, and very often, that place is filled by a grateful guest privileged to eat my mother's cooking and experience my parents' continued generosity. During the meals in which that extra seat is not filled, it continues to serve as a reminder of a Jewish value that has survived thousands of years, countless persecutions, and endless wandering. Wherever we eat, there is always room for one more.

Honoring Those Who Came Before

Paradise

Seth Schindler

There were no pogroms or death camps in the Borscht Belt.

In the Borscht Belt of my youth, the 1950s, there was pinball and summer camp. We feasted on borscht, sweet and sour, the story of our people. Tummlers like Mel Brooks helped us to forget—for a while anyway.

The dramatic change of scenery was another attraction, an escape from gritty New York City to summertime Eden. We reveled in its verdant mountain vistas, pine-scented fresh air, and pristine streams and lakes.

But it was more. We could be ourselves, feel the power of community and reconnect with our ancient noble roots.

It was Paradise for us: the survivors, their children and grandchildren.

I was ten years old. Standing behind the counter on a wooden box, I took a nickel out of the cash register. I was about to pocket it and close the cash register drawer when I saw my Aunt Silvia and froze. She was coming out of the kitchen of the lodge my extended family operated in the Catskills in the summer of 1957. It served several nearby summer bungalow colonies around a lake in the town of Loch Sheldrake. The tarnished metal counter was the soda fountain of my dreams. There I drank endless egg creams, black-and-white ice cream sodas and chocolate malteds. The groceries and home supplies that we sold at cost lined the shelves behind it. The profit center sustaining that loss leader strategy took some chutzpah to pull off: the gambling parlor disguised as a dining room.

"Halten!" Aunt Sylvia shouted.

I dropped the nickel back into the cash register and hopped off the box.

Hands on her wide hips, Aunt Sylvia stared at me. "Stealing . . . and from mishpokhe, no less. What are you, a goy? And gambling too, with those stupid machines."

I walked rapidly around the counter into the lobby where the pinball machines were. "It's not real gambling, Aunt Sylvia. *That* is." I pointed to the gambling room off the lobby, where men were playing poker and pinochle, as they did every Saturday night, and where women played mahjong weekday afternoons. They loved to gamble as much as the men.

"Don't be such a smartass," Aunt Sylivia said.

"I'm sick of being called that." I leaned against my favorite pinball machine, Marble Queen. I liked it because it had a "double award" option if you played two coins. Or maybe it was that the graphics featured gorgeous young blond women in skimpy bathing suits—*Shiksas*, according to the recently bar-mitzvahed David, the camp's resident expert on such things.

Sylvia walked slowly around the counter and sat on a stool. "Then stop acting like one."

"Why do Jewish people love to gamble so much?" I had already learned how effective changing the subject quickly could be when you're in trouble.

"Why do you constantly ask questions? Ask your mother." Sylvia turned toward Roana, my mother, who'd just entered the lobby pushing a hand truck that held a case of seltzer bottles, the old-fashioned kind with metal syphons.

"Because we're very good at gambling," Roana sighed. "Better than anyone else. We had to be, to survive. Risky business, easy to fail at, was the only kind of work the goyim ever allowed us to do."

I ran my hand across the glass top of Marble Queen. "Gambling's fun too, I bet. Like pinball." When I wasn't at day camp, I played the game like there was no tomorrow. Not that I was the Pinball Wizard, but I did play a mean pinball and had quite a rep. When Henny Youngman once came to perform at our lodge, he even asked me to teach him how to play.

Roana nodded and lit a Pall Mall. "But it can and should be more. The kind of challenge you need to take, if you're a mensch. Smart enough to know that's the way you learn best."

"Learn what?"

Roana smiled, something she rarely did. "How to outsmart the goyim."

Aunt Sylivia laughed. "Listen to your mother, she's real good at that."

"Why should I outsmart them?" I asked Roana.

Roana's fierce dark eyes narrowed. "Zol er krenken un gedenken."

"What does that mean?" My parents wouldn't let me speak Yiddish, though gradually I picked up some.

Roana took a long drag on her cigarette. "Mean . . . shmean. A curse they deserve. For what they've done to us."

"What was that? I want to know."

Roana pushed the hand truck next to me. "Better to know this, my boychik. Never be afraid to take a chance in your life. To do what others think is too difficult or are too scared to do. Maybe you'll fail. But so what? You'll learn more that way. Now take this seltzer and go help your father with the cocktails. Where the real gelt is. Too bad our tribe doesn't drink like the goyim. And remember what I told you. Keep your mouth shut in there. And if you can't, try to say something nice for a change. Better yet, just smile like your father does."

I dropped my head, afraid to look into the eyes of the force of nature that was my dear mother. "But that smile of his is fake."

"For this I survived . . . what wasn't fake?"

"*What* wasn't?" I looked up. My mother's eyes were closed.

"Never mind," she muttered as she turned and walked away.

I pushed the hand truck into the gambling parlor where I saw Gene, my father, smiling as usual, that familiar frozen grin that always bothered me. He reminded me of one of those scary clowns, with a mysterious darkness lurking behind their smiles. Years later, I saw Gene greeting guests at his restaurant on Broadway in Manhattan, the famous Hawaii Kai. His smile, if you could call it that, by then had nothing enigmatic in it. What I saw in it and his eyes was only sadness.

"Take this gin and tonic to the Pickle King," Gene said to me.

I glared at him. "I don't want to. Shimmy's always making fun of me and my you know what. Pointing a big dill pickle at it and laughing."

"Shimmy's just a kibitzer, Seth. Don't take him . . . what he says or does . . . seriously."

I scanned the room filled with our kind of royalty. At every table there was at least one king. Former street peddlers who'd made it big. Kenny the Kugel King. Moe the Knish Macher. And, of course, our family's own king, my Uncle Irving, the biggest of them all, the Pretzel King of Brooklyn.

"They're all like that," I said. "Think they're so funny. Why do they make everything into a joke?"

He put his arm around me, pulled me close and kissed me on the lips. "It's just their way of dealing with all the *tsuris* they've . . . we've . . . known. One day you'll understand. It's complicated. Ask your mother."

Roana never helped me understand, either. She, like all my older relatives, and many other immigrant Jews of that generation, would never talk about their lives in the old country.

Her only response to my persistent questions about our family's past was that Yiddish curse I later learned means, *May they suffer and remember.* I didn't understand her anger then. Now I do.

Researchers at the Holocaust Memorial Museum helped me find where Roana's family had lived in the "old country." The old Jewish ghetto of the city of Borshchiv, in what is now Ukraine. I wanted to visit it. But they advised me not to. All I'd find was a memorial inscribed with a Star of David, and this:

To the Memory of the Thousands of Jews Murdered Here by the Nazis.

I didn't understand my father's sadness then. Now I do. What I discovered only recently when I googled "Schindler's," the name of the hotel his family owned a century ago, was that it was one of the first Borscht Belt hotels serving Jews from New York City, at a time when many upstate and elsewhere closed their doors to them.

This is where Gene spent his childhood. Until the hotel burned to the ground in 1926. The horrific fire accidentally started, according to an article in the local newspaper, by the owner's ten-year old son. Eugene Schindler. It killed many of its occupants, including the owner. Samuel Schindler. The tragedy must have haunted my father the rest of his life.

The Hebrew name for Samuel is Shimshon. The Hebrew name I was given.

They and all their kings are gone now, as is that magical summer world.

If there is a Paradise, maybe, just maybe, it's another Borscht Belt. A better world for them all year long. A place where they can eat borscht—only sweet this time around—to their heart's content. Where Mel Brooks is always there to make them laugh and they finally find the peace they never knew.

This Isn't About a Bracelet
Melinda Gordon Blum

I'm taking a shower when I first notice it's missing—the beautiful antique gold, rectangular-link chain bracelet that once belonged to Magdalena (Magda), my father's mother. The one I haven't taken off my wrist since my mom gave it to me five years ago, shortly after Dad died. Mom has scant details regarding how the bracelet survived when its owner did not. So much of my family's history falls into this category.

Mom thinks when my grandmother Magda was deported from Budapest to Dachau, she left some valuables behind for safekeeping with my great-aunt Judit and my great-uncle Miklós, Magda's brother. Judit and Miklós managed to hold onto these items until after the war, but no one alive knows how. And how the jewelry came into Dad's possession is another mystery. He couldn't have taken his mother's jewelry when he first fled Hungary, as he wasn't even able to alert his family before his escape. Dad must have smuggled it out (under communism, it was illegal to remove valuables from the country), or taken it later, legally, once Hungary was no longer under Soviet rule.

I towel off, pull on yesterday's jeans and a clean t-shirt, and run back to my bedroom, wet hair dripping a trail across the hardwood. Is the bracelet in the sheets? I shake them gently, listening for rustling sounds. Is it on the floor? I get down on my stomach and shine my iPhone flashlight under the bed. I see dust balls, a charging cord, and a sock, but no bracelet. I mentally check off the places I went yesterday: the boys' high school. The car wash. A movie theater. When did I last have it?

It could be anywhere.

It is nowhere.

I plop down on the fluffy white area rug (no bracelet there) and cry. It feels childish, embarrassing, to be crying over a bracelet. It has sentimental value. Monetary value. But in the end, it is just a bracelet—a bauble, a thing. The sooner I accept I'll never see it again, the better off I'll be. I'm wiping my tears when I remember something I once heard: "When people argue about who left the cap off the toothpaste, it's never about the toothpaste."

This isn't about a bracelet.

August 4, 2017, the day the bracelet goes missing, is the five-year anniversary of my father's death. Not a day goes by when I am not reminded of him. Amidst the madness of the current political environment, I think about how he was a Holocaust survivor. Every time a disturbing story about Jews becomes a news item, I wonder what he'd say about the resurgence in antisemitism. I'm reminded of him in the beautiful music my boys play on their guitars, and on the baby grand piano that once was his. I see an echo of my father in my younger son's mathematical ability, which he certainly didn't inherit from me. My older son's facial features, as he matures, are becoming more and more like Dad's image in old family photographs.

As the years pass, it's harder to resist the urge to mythologize my father—to think of him in the broad strokes of his many contributions to the Jewish community. He was a person who did a lot of good, so much so that sometimes the legacy he's left behind feels intimidating. Though he was one of my biggest cheerleaders, I'm not sure I'm up to the task of returning the favor. Do I measure up? Am I capable of doing his memory justice?

When self-doubt weighs me down, it's because my father's larger-than-life reputation distances me from who he actually was. It saddens me, how much he is already receding. The sound of his voice, his facial expressions, and his mannerisms are fading from memory. The funny bark of his laugh. The rare, syntactical reveal, aside from his accent, that English was his second language, like how he'd ask his grandsons if they'd remembered to "wash their hand" before dinner. The way he said hello and goodbye European style, kissing us on both cheeks. The pieces that composed him as a man, as my father, are becoming more difficult to conjure. Which parts are made up? Which parts are real?

The bracelet is a tangible thing. It exists. It holds within it a kind of solidity and certainty. It is something I can point to—something here in this world, now, not floating around inside the capricious clouds of oral histories and flawed memory. It is a filament connecting me not just to the past but to my people. My grandmother, who was murdered by Nazis more than twenty years before I was born, once wore it around her wrist. It's all I had of her. It's the closest I'll ever come to holding her hand. Maybe I expected too much. Maybe I expected it to be a rope thrown to a woman overboard. It's just a delicate, gossamer thing. A thing that somehow, improbably, survived when her flesh and bone could not.

I ground myself, sometimes, by homing in on some of the smaller characteristics I've inherited. I share Dad's nerdy love of wordplay. I, too, am a connoisseur of gallows humor (days before he lapsed into a coma, he was still cracking his trademark deadpan jokes). I got his news and NPR addiction and his caffeine addiction, too. He hooked me on coffee as a child, offering me sugar cubes dipped in espresso whenever we visited our Hungarian relatives. And … there is also how calm and focused I am when faced with the prospect of big problems but how absolutely over-the-top freaked out I become when I lose or misplace something.

This isn't about a bracelet.

I drive to Mount Sinai Cemetery near Griffith Park. It is midmorning. On the rolling, emerald green hills, the automatic sprinklers are on, spraying water in arcing circles: TCK TCK TCK. Gardeners fan out across the acres of grounds, weed whackers edging the grass between the plots and leaf blowers droning like swarms of angry bees. The smell of gasoline thickens the already humid air. A growing disappointment rumbles in my belly. On the drive over, I imagined sitting peacefully by Dad's headstone. I'd inhale air that was crisp and clear and sweet. I'd listen to an occasional birdsong, feel a gentle breeze rustling through the trees. I pictured a perfect, meaningful moment. A respite from my frantic morning. The kind of experience that never measures up in real life to the visions I hold in my head.

I wish I could wrap this up by telling you that I call the movie theater, and my bracelet is waiting for me in the Lost & Found. Or that I get back to my car and see a glimmer in a crevice by the driver's seat. I love these endings. They provide a nice sense of closure.

Sometimes, though, we lose things we assume will be with us forever. And we learn how to go on without them.

This isn't about a bracelet.

I have another piece of jewelry that belonged to Dad's uncle. He helped raise Dad after his parents died. It's a gold signet ring that bears the initials MV. Miklós Vali. Despite the delicate engraved flowers on its sides, it's a masculine ring, substantial, square and chunky. I wear it on my right middle finger. Miklós must have worn it on his pinky. That's how I picture it, anyway. When I have it on, the heavy ring feels like a divining rod—as though it's pulling me towards the earth. I have a story about that, too. Somehow this gravitational force carries a message from my father's soul. *You are safe*, I imagine him saying. *You are grounded. This ring connects you to the core of our family. And so it also connects you to your best self.*

Maybe the bracelet story ends with tuning out the weed-whacking, leaf-blowing gardeners for a minute. That's all the time I need to reread the Anne Frank quote my mother, sister, and I chose for my father's headstone. *A single candle*, it says, etched in script into the beautiful, sun-warmed, reddish-brown marble, *can both defy and define the darkness.*

My dad's light is gone. Or, maybe more accurately, it's passed along. Energy never dies, I hear. It gets repurposed. Maybe I already have all the things I want and need. I am not obligated to let go of the stories that console me. I can choose to believe Dad's light is still defying and defining the darkness. It's just doing so in a new way.

All I can do is be a single candle. That's not too much to ask of anybody. That is enough.

I think I can do it. I hope I can. I'll try.

A Toy Soldier Named "Papa"

Melissa Greenwood

> I the Lord have called unto you in righteousness, and have taken hold of your hand, and submitted you as the people's covenant, as a light unto the nations.
>
> —Isaiah 42:6

A toy soldier sits on my kitchen windowsill—a dusty memento from my grandfather's 100th birthday party, three Octobers ago. Appropriately, he's army green: two inches long by half an inch wide. Legs akimbo, helmet on, and gun in hand, the figurine is the same size as my forearm tattoos and as hard as my delicate, flower-themed ink is soft.

It strikes me that, like Papa, my body art was born of hardness—from tiny rose- and peony-shaped jabs by a mighty needle. For my grandpa, this harshness was the prick of the world. His earliest years included the loss of one sister to childhood illness and the backdrop of the Great Depression—both of which shaped him into a tough, scrappy kid who found himself enlisting.

But no matter how many photos I've seen of him dressed smartly in his uniform, I can't reconcile the adoring grandfather I love with the young man he was—hard and ready for battle as this warring figurine.

Two Chanukahs ago, when Papa was still strong, he gazed at me wistfully as though a century-plus of life flashed before him. When a sentimental look washed over him, I knew he was not only reflecting backward, but also thinking forward. He was seeing present-me and imagining future-me in a future he wouldn't live to see. He was remembering all my firsts and wondering about his lasts.

§

It's February now, and another Chanukah has passed. But not Papa. Not yet. As I write this at his hospice bedside, I watch a vaporizer bubble steam through an elephant tusk. It's quiet for the moment, save for the whir and hum of the oxygen machine, but last week brought a wheezing cough, and earlier today, we met the death rattle: a gurgling noise like someone calling for help underwater. But that couldn't be Papa—he's too strong a swimmer. Or at least he was before three back-to-back falls left him bedridden.

Even after a decade of congestive heart failure, even after four broken ribs and a fractured hip, even after four days without food or water, Papa manages labored breaths through his wide-open mouth, and I can't help but think of the phrase *soldiering on*. My grandfather fought the Nazis. Of course he's fighting death.

He stirs reflexively as nurses, family members, and palliative care workers buzz around him. To the right of me, the kitchen's accordion doors slide open and closed as more relatives prepare to eat leftovers off mismatched flatware. I flip through the news to pass the time and learn we're on day 492 of Israel at war. Flashing before me are the images of three recently released hostages—gaunt and emaciated as any we've seen. I'm startled by how much these hollow-cheeked, sunken-eyed men resemble my skeletal grandpa. Sarcopenia, they call it. Muscle wasting.

I close my computer like a book.

My grandmother stands beside Papa and says the Shema. Says *we're all here, honey. It's okay. We'll be okay.* She takes his swollen, purple hand as the hospice aide administers more liquid morphine. They keep shortening the window between doses—four hours, three hours, two. It strikes me that the caretaker moves between the couch and Papa's bedside as unobtrusively as a seasoned server might, only he's not swapping out a dull fork for a shiny one. He's filling and emptying syringes, hoping to make Papa more comfortable.

Ten months ago, Papa and I were interviewed by the local news. They were doing a segment on the Israel-Hamas war, and I had just returned from a week of volunteering in Israel—a week made possible by Papa's generosity when he slipped me some money for airfare, the way grandpas sometimes do. While my voice kept catching as I shared about wanting to be of service and feeling called to come forward—my own mini-version of enlisting—Papa's voice was clear and strong, even on the topic of antisemitism. I fell apart that day, but my ever-resilient grandfather kept it together. Now, with his 103-year-old body failing him, he's the one falling apart.

I open my computer to jot down this reflection: Defying death and eradicating the oldest hatred in the world are both losing battles.

§

Last Shabbat, we finally lost our family patriarch. *It's time to go now, Larry. We love you, Larry. Just relax and let go,* my grandmother urged in hushed tones, and he listened. He was wearing blue socks, and I was holding his sweet, flat foot in my hand as his soul made its ascent. Those flat feet could have excused Papa from service eighty-three years ago, but that's not who my grandfather was. He lived his Jewish values with those feet, walking through the world (and no doubt into the next) with exceptional integrity.

This Shabbat, before I make my way to shul to say the Kaddish, I do as Jewish women have for generations: I welcome the Sabbath bride with familiar Hebrew words and the strike of a match. Kindling the candles takes me back to the Festival of Lights, not this past December—when Papa's spark had all but dimmed—but the one before it. I smile, remembering the sound of ancient prayers on his weathered lips. With the New York accent he tried but failed to disguise, he was chanting the Chanukah blessings but thinking, I imagine, about the blessing of family—his own younger face reflected back at him in each of ours, like the reflection of this much-needed Shabbos light off my kitchen windows.

"It's time to leave for temple," my husband calls from the other room, interrupting my reverie. Only, the toy soldier calls to me, too. I pick him up and stroke him gently, the very way I rubbed Papa's tired feet. *Thank you,* I whisper to the figurine as softly as Grandma whispered her last words to our real soldier, now finally at rest.

Thank you for living to tuck away your rifle.
Thank you for the legacy of your wonderfully wrinkled life.
Thank you for being the brightest of Jewish lights.

Jewish Joy Stuffed in My Suitcase
Ana Miriam Lublin

I was travelling from California to Copenhagen with my fiancée Katrine to have our big-fat Jewish-Danish wedding!

The day before, I had spun in confusion, having no idea what to pack. I stuffed my luggage with silver high heels, scuffed black waterproof boots, t-shirts, a purple raincoat, a red puffy windbreaker, jeans, jogging pants and too much makeup. But there was zero confusion about bringing my most treasured carry-on: my resilient Jewish ancestors, who would join me on this exhausting and exhilarating 20-hour flight.

Would the Jewish spirit be accepted in the little land with only three thousand Jews? Most Danes had never met a Jew. Denmark was a place with soft candles, cozy and hygge. And church weddings that repeated the same Christian rituals. I have always been a loud and proud Jew. But I was about to have my first spirited-wild–public Jewish celebration.

I was breaking their rules.

With adrenaline coursing through my body, we made it to the San Francisco International Airport. The luggage conveyor whirred as I dropped my suitcase onto the belt. I held onto my purple carry-on backpack, in which I'd shoved my uncertainty, hidden amongst a journal and bags of salty almonds.

At security, the stern guard beeped the silver wand over my body. Stay calm, I told myself.

The terminal was a dizzying sea of humanity, the sweet, sugary scents of cinnamon rolls and donuts wafting in the air. I pulled my journal out of my backpack, and we wrote our wedding vows. My vow number 1: I promise never to leave the apartment without red lipstick. Katrine's vow number 1:

She promised never to make me leave the apartment without red lipstick. We laughed hysterically, like giddy adolescents.

As a lonely teenager, I would lie in bed eating Snickers bars and dream about getting married in a green dress. Chewing on the salty peanuts and sweet milk chocolate, I pictured us kissing under a protective chuppah. After I smashed the glass with my spiked heels, guests would cheer "Mazel Tov!" My grandparents would be verklempt. I could not have imagined this crazy blend of ancient Jewish and Viking traditions. Now this new dream was taking flight.

At the gate, a tall blonde Scandinavian announced, "Zone 3 boarding now." Sweat slicked my palms.

It all felt like a miracle.

My very existence came about from tiny choices—and pure luck. One slip, and I would not have been born. In 1943 Poland, my family lived in the Lodz Ghetto as Hitler was closing in. Grandpa went through hell at Buchenwald, but he escaped from a death march. The Nazis mercilessly ripped my seven-year-old dad away from his parents. But Grandma Dora, sick to her bones, lied to the Germans about my dad's age, telling them he was older than he was. Because of her razor's edge choice, Dad ended up under Luba, the Angel of Bergen Belsen's care. Luba flirted with the Nazis, so she was able to procure more food for her charges than most children in the camps would ever receive. Grandma was enslaved in Bergen-Belsen and did not know if my dad was alive. All three barely survived. When liberation came in 1945, they were reunited. Their starved bodies could finally touch each other again.

Indomitable survival genes were lodged deep inside of me.

Grandpa Michal passed away at the age of eighty-five. Grandma was still a force of nature at ninety-four. But my Bubbie was too exhausted to travel the five thousand miles to our wedding. Mom, Dad, and my big brother made up the tiny crew of Jewish family members flying in to celebrate.

Katrine's story was the opposite of mine. She was born in Denmark, and with the adventurousness of a Viking, she left her safe country at eighteen. Warm, sun-drenched California beckoned. Her huge clan stayed in their freezing nation. She had hundreds of relatives, who were about to witness their first Jewish wedding. Excitement and curiosity bubbled through my in-laws.

Katrine's mother grabbed us at the Copenhagen airport. After one night of rest, we drove over to the spacious white building in the middle of Copenhagen.

Finally, our big day had arrived.

The clock struck one, leaving us two hours to get ready. I floated over my body in a dissociated haze and watched myself slip on sheer stockings and pull on my sparkly green dress with just enough cleavage to feel sexy. I dipped into red lipstick, rouge, and eyeshadow and painted my face. Silver glittery high heels matched my silver glittery shawl. I transformed into the glowing fairy bride I'd wanted to be since I was young. Draped in wedding garb, I was transported from the mundane to the magical. Grandma and Grandpa, I whispered, please come with me.

The clock struck three. My stomach fluttered as we walked down the aisle. I landed under the glistening homemade pink chuppah, bursting with red and white silk flowers. Danes sat on the edge of their seats, slack jawed. Jewish rituals mixed with our tongue-in-cheek vows. Katrine and I exchanged ten-dollar bubble-gum-machine rings. Guests cried and laughed as a friend recited a fairytale about the origins of our love: I met Katrine on a blind date and was immediately charmed.

I stomped my heel, shattering the glass hidden under a white cloth. I raised my hands in the air, triumphant. A few lonely *Mazel Tov*s rang out from my little family and one Jewish friend. The Danes' eyes shone with light. Katrine and I skipped down the aisle giggling. The festivities began.

Everyone feasted on fish, chicken, grated beet salad, and chocolate cake. We were gifted hilarious speeches and songs the Danes wrote for us. Katrine's brother composed a mini operetta. Friends dressed up in hippie garb and sang a funky, feminist folk song. Katrine laughed so hard she spit out her wine. Danes clinked silverware on their wine glasses, their tradition commanding that we stand on chairs and kiss each other. Teetering, we carefully smooched our lipstick away. We ate marzipan, and the chocolate coconut dessert melted on our tongues. Champagne was spilled, and the tables glowed with stunning white flowers. As we were eating, two men ran over to Katrine, brandishing large silver swords.

"What are you doing to my wife?" I screamed. With their enormous blades, the grinning men sliced off the toes of her socks. The Danes were stopping "the groom" from running away and cheating. "Your people are as meshuga as mine," I told Katrine, my head in my hands.

Suddenly, a violin note beckoned in a minor key. Bow and string trembled, conversations halted. Seduced by the siren's song, we turned towards the band. The Klezmer music began slowly, softly, then rose and quickened. We swayed and tapped to the lively beat.

My eyes landed on my father, huddled with his second wife at a table.

"Dad," I called out, "It is time to lead the dance!"

And with his mop of salt and pepper curls and slim figure, Dad led us in Israeli folk dancing. One hundred people clasped hands and wove through the dark room. The glass chandeliers shook, as we lit up the room with huge smiles.

Then I became a Jewish queen, hoisted up on a chair, bouncing above my beautiful community. When I was placed back on the ground, I threw off my heels and danced defiantly.

I danced for my grandparents who fought for me to have this life. I danced for the Danish Resistance that saved seven thousand Jews during World War II.

I danced for the perseverance of my people.

Hours later, the clock struck 3 a.m., and most of the stragglers had gone home. I was wilting, ready to collapse into bed. But my tall, twenty-year-old Dansk nephew-in-law Lasse was still hanging onto the night. His thick blonde hair swooped over his forehead and his dark brown eyes shone. Bursting with enthusiasm he exclaimed, "That was amazing. I really want to have a Jewish wedding."

He hugged me tightly.

My exhaustion faded. With my hands on my hips, I looked him straight in the eyes and smiled.

Filled with pride, I declared, "Jewish joy is contagious." And I knew. The spirit of my ancestors lived indelibly inside of me. A gift I could bring anywhere.

The Power of the Plastic Fork

Debbie Feit

By the time I reached junior high, my observant Jewish father recognized that my keeping kosher would have to be my decision, and I recognized that McDonald's chicken nuggets were far superior to the Filet-O-Fish sandwich. Still, we kept a kosher home, separate dishes and utensils for meat and dairy, and at any given time, sentinels of silverware were holding their posts in the kitchen flowerpots, my parents' attempt to render now sullied utensils kosher again after what was often my mishap of using a meat spoon to eat ice cream.

Although ours was a kosher home—no pork, no shellfish, certainly no cheeseburgers—my father kept a work schedule that would include the occasional dinner meeting, which gave my less observant mother the opportunity to take my sister and me out for shrimp parmigiana at the Italian restaurant or sweet and sour chicken from the non-kosher Chinese place, which was not all that different from the sweet and sour chicken we got from the kosher Chinese place. The major difference was that it wasn't kosher, which to my sister and me felt forbidden and exciting and therefore far more delicious. We'd bring it back to our house and eat it on paper plates with plastic forks to preserve the kosher status of our kitchen. My father's Judaism, including his commitment to keeping kosher, was an essential part of his being, as was his respect for the different choices I would make throughout mine: marrying a Presbyterian, joining a Reform synagogue rather than a Conservative one, celebrating Christmas with my in-laws.

My father's Judaism remained essential up until the end of his life, when he collapsed on his way to the Western Wall in Jerusalem, a more fitting ending to such a devoted man I could not have scripted myself. After his funeral, after sitting *shiva,* after the initial, but by no means final, flood of grief and tears and sleepless nights, I returned to his home and packed up the prayer books he used for daily services and gathered the yarmulkes my mother made--crocheted keepsakes of my father's beloved Judaism. I took his collection of *Chai* necklaces and Hebrew-name rings for safekeeping in my drawer and made sure his many *tallit* found suitable homes with his daughters and grandchildren and nieces.

I filled more than fifty banker boxes with his books and researched places that might be interested in the ones about Judaism and Israel, the old, oversized prayer books, and the one published in 1878 that I imagined had once belonged to my grandfather. All of them were treasures I had no idea existed. I had no idea they had been living on his bookshelves for all these years and no idea if I would have been as interested in hearing about them were my father still alive to tell me. I cancelled his cell phone and looked for a buyer interested in midcentury modern bedroom furniture. I found Father's Day gifts my sister and I had given him as children, a set of linen napkins with my great-grandmother's monogram, and the folders he and my mother had been keeping for decades that were filled with my college projects, receipts to vendors from my wedding to the Presbyterian, magazine pages featuring both ads and articles I had written over the years.

I found all this and much more and wondered if I'd ever find the right words to put on his headstone, a task I had been assigned as I was a writer and had been my entire professional life. This would be the second time I would be challenged with the assignment no child, writer or not, wants to receive. In between packing the books, making the phone calls, and being amused at the discovery of the catering menu from my wedding reception (which was not a kosher affair but still afforded plenty of options for those who observed, my father particularly enthralled by the selection of mushroom appetizers we offered as part of the cocktail hour), I worked remotely from my father's dining room table.

The night before I flew back home, I ordered takeout shrimp and pasta from the Italian place near his house. I ate from the container with a plastic fork, despite the fact that a full selection of silverware still remained in the drawers, both meat and dairy, but certainly no silverware allocated for non-kosher. I used a plastic fork because I was overcome by a desire to maintain my father's kosher kitchen, a desire that was as unexpected as his death. I wanted to preserve the *kashrut* of his silverware even though I knew his silverware and his dishes and his pots and pans would be donated to people in need of such things, to people who didn't necessarily need such things to be kosher. Still, I ate my shrimp and pasta with a plastic fork and kept his fork kosher, kept his kitchen kosher, kept everything kosher even though nothing was kosher, nothing okay about the fact that he was gone. By keeping his fork and his kitchen kosher, it was still his. It was still his and he was still there with me.

My Father's Floating Burial

Amy Shimshon-Santo

> "When I write, I try to be loyal to the dream, not the circumstances."
> —Jose Luis Borges

My Pop exists in the ether like a weathervane. Gone but also present. I feel him as a subtle, guiding accompaniment. David died ten years ago. One day I will too. I understand death as a natural part of the mystery of life. Since death will happen to all of us, we might as well talk about it.

When I was 18, Pop took me to visit his father for the last time. I was a dancer, living in New York, and זיידע was at an elder care facility in New Jersey. When we found him, he was resting on a rolling gurney in a cotton hospital gown. A plastic receptacle for collecting urine hung from the frame. His belly that I'd remembered as pronounced was deflated. His body was still as a slab of breathing wood.

Pop stood beside זיידע and caressed his kepele of thin white hair, just as he would a small child's. I watched them communicating in a wordless language of care. Time slowed down as I witnessed their shifting roles. Tenderness. Delicacy. Humility.

When the visit was over, we left the quiet room to walk toward the exit. The soles of our shoes clicked in unison along the slick institutional floor.

This is where they put all the old people, I remember thinking. *That's why we don't see them.*

The doors opened automatically. Brisk air crisped the skin of my face and hands. Emotions were coursing through me, unable to find an outlet in language. I foraged through my brain seeking the right words for my father.

"Jelly omelette?" I said.

Our jelly omelettes were a blend of butter, eggs, and strawberry jam. It was the signature meal he'd prepared for me when I was a kid. Pop grinned knowingly, pleased that I remembered his acts of kindness. Now, I could be the one to fill his plate instead of the other way around.

I grew up in California, far away from our kin in New Jersey, Tel Aviv, Canada, and Uruguay. Distance impacted my experience of family rituals, including end of life. I have never attended a funeral for either of my parents' families. You only have 24 hours to bury the dead, and it might have taken us longer just to arrive. I've never visited a cemetery for my father's people. Granted, he was first generation born in the U.S., and his family in the Pale of Settlement was murdered without regard to their humanity.

The cemeteries of my mother's people stay open 24/7. They're surrounded by tall trees with scraggly branches resembling the beards of pious men pointing skyward. When I arrive in the Middle East, someone in the family invariably asks me if I will go with them to the cemetery. It's a place of perpetual prayer and candle lighting. Believe me, people are there right now jotting down wishes on scraps of paper and pushing them between stones. The living are scavenging rocks to remember their dead.

Gravestones are sardined together, charted numerically and alphabetically, to help you find them. For example, M-6 or B-12. Bingo! Rows of unadorned slate, chiseled with Hebrew letters, serve as markers of memory. All that matters is if you were good. We are the children of people, and, sometimes, the progenitors of people. Once, when I went with my cousin to visit the tablet for our סבא רבא רבא (great great grandfather Alter Shloime Noach), a wild leafy plant climbed upward from his rock.

My father did not believe in cemeteries. He wanted land to be used for affordable housing. One day he handed me his blue Neptune Society identity card and said when the time comes "have them haul it away." His wish made sense, but, of course, was not Halacha. When we die, our bodies are to be wrapped in cotton and laid humbly in the earth. But death has become an industry that Pop wanted no part of. He prioritized the living.

When Pop died, his phrase glowed neon in my memory. *Just have them haul it away.* Don't be attached to the physical. When grief infiltrated me,

I remembered his dictate as a lesson. His challenge to think of him as an "it" felt matter-of-fact, almost comical. *Don't think of my body as who I am.* Maybe he was something else.

As I enter my elder years, I realize that unless something unimaginable happens, one thing I may lose in the United States is a burial. They are hard to finance, and, even if I could, there is no one in the family to be next to.

Anyone who has been through grief knows it feels all encompassing.

"If you don't know how to do it," my mother said, "there are people who will come and cry for you."

When Pop died, I learned that I can grieve on demand very well. I cried like a sandstorm. A real pro.

Other than my capacity for weeping I felt completely analfabeta, or illiterate, about dying. Thankfully, our end of life rituals also include sitting shiva and reciting the kaddish. Pop's shiva attracted a week of non-stop visitations from the community. Storytelling. Food. Tears. Hugs. You're too sad to do anything else, so why not hang out with loved ones and share memories? Talking story as a community helps us piece together the bigger picture of someone's life. The parts you knew, and the parts you did not. In addition to the shiva, I always am comforted by standing together and speaking the names of our loved ones when the shofar blows during high holidays. Each year we also light yahrzeit candles to rekindle memories.

On the last day of Pop's shiva, an email arrived from him in my inbox that read simply "Amy. Test." A few days later, he appeared in my dream as a young person in swimming trunks standing beside a melting porcelain bust of his former self. He was bouncing eagerly, up and down on his metatarsals. Pop came to say a quick hello before meeting his friends to swim the seas. Pop had put himself through school, working as a lifeguard. I liked knowing that he was swimming again.

Then nothing. Years passed without a sign. We had honored his wish, but I longed for a place to go and sit with his memory. A gravesite. *Where do I set a stone for my father?* My animal emotions wanted this.

One night I awoke to the sound of chanting. A group of hassidic rabbis surrounding my Pop's deceased body levitated in the air above my bed.

Chochma! Chochma!, they chanted in unison.

Dressed in black coats, trousers, and brimmed hats with white shirts, tzitzit, and yarmulkes, the rabbis were laser focused. They sprinkled sand on his body and spoke to his soul with a word from the sephirot that means wisdom. I sensed right away they were spiritually caring for whatever Pop had argued was his "it" — the lifelessness he had wanted hauled off.

Chochma! Chochma!, the rabbis chanted.

The lead rabbi was the eldest and smallest. Silver beard. Encyclopedia of a man. He captivated everyone's attention, guiding every minute detail of the team's actions.

This went on for quite some time. I get out of bed.

Chochma!

I walk to the bathroom.

Chochma!

I wash my hands, just like we do before leaving a cemetery.

Chochma!

I return to the bedroom.

Chochma!

They are still at it. A sky full of sound with precise ritual movements.

I get back into bed and decide to just give them space to do whatever it is they need to do for Pop. The sephirot are the sephirot. The tree of life goes deeper than anything my rational mind could possibly grasp. Eventually, my eyes close.

I never saw them leave. In the morning, there was nothing above me but the ceiling. Refreshed, and a bit perplexed, I wondered what might have inspired this event. Maybe Pop had earned sky cred from serving as Rabbi Prinz's bal Torah when he was a boy. Maybe it was the spiritual request from his father, Shloime from Pitkamien. Maybe his great grandfather Israel Dov Rosenbaum, the paper cutter, had wanted this done. Maybe it was the wish of his grandfather Piotr, the bolshevik who wove horsehair necklaces from prison mattresses in Tsarist Russia. Maybe it was his mother Reva, the pianist and peace activist, who had set the ritual into motion. Maybe the whole mysterious event was just his good luck, a destiny he'd earned from being a mensch.

All I know is somehow, what was done was finally done. His soul was cared for by the many souls who came before us. "It" was complete.

Tell Me Another One
Rochelle Newman-Carrasco

There once was a hoo-er from Peru
Who filled her vagina with glue
She said with a grin, if they pay to get in
They'll pay to get out of there too.

My 84-year-old grandmother giggled, pleased with herself. The seder meal had ended and the post-meal Haggadah reading had not yet begun. Given that my father conducted the entire seder in both Hebrew and English, and encouraged discussion, debate and digressions, it was a long night. Comic relief was always welcome.

"Tell another one, Nana," I begged.

She was just getting started. My grandmother's repertoire of dirty jokes in both Yiddish, and Lower-East-Side-New-York-accented English, was infamous. But my Catholic Panamanian-born boyfriend Carlos, who would go on to become my husband, had yet to experience anything like it.

"There was a boy and a girl, and they were fucking..."

My grandmother launched into a longer off-color joke with the precision and timing of a polished stand-up comic. I found it impossible to retell them with her accuracy and spirit. Why I never recorded her, I don't know. She wasn't just being funny, she used humor to create bonds. Although I didn't learn Yiddish, I never grew tired of hearing her rattle off jokes I couldn't understand but could feel. The guttural *ch's*. The faintly understandable phrases like *vi geyt biznes?* And the almost edible consonant combos as in *Shlekht, tzu leygn,* and *nisht geferlach.*

As each joke resolved, she would break out into a contagious laugh, look me in the eye and ask, *farshteyst?* Understand? And even though I didn't, I did.

My mother could have learned my grandmother's jokes but chose not to. Or if she did know them, she kept that to herself. There was a tension in their relationship that kept the two women at odds. A joke-telling session, whether you're the comic or the audience, has a certain intimacy. Laughter is love. But my mother couldn't allow herself to be that vulnerable in front of her own mother.

When my grandmother met Carlos, my aunt asked her what she thought. "Well," she said before an extended pause. "He's very *tawl*." That, it turned out, was an endorsement. By not saying anything critical, by staying neutral to nice, she was giving her approval.

My father had given Carlos a Spanish-language Haggadah, his way of making sense of my out-of-religion relationship. This gift followed my father's explanation of how Carlos's surname, Carrasco, was a crypto-Jewish name. Pre-internet, he would never say how he knew this to be so, but post-internet, it would prove to be true. The Carrasco name is on a list of crypto-Jewish names—those Jews who survived the Spanish Inquisition by professing another religion publicly, while practicing Judaism in secret. To keep children out of danger, true identities were also kept secret while some rituals, like lighting candles, spinning "tops" near Christmastime, and placing six-pointed-stars on tombstones, remained. As time passed, the rituals were no longer part of a hidden identity. They simply were.

It should be noted that Carlos had no need for a Spanish-language Haggadah. His English was not only perfect, but he had majored in Classical Theater and Rhetoric, advancing to post-graduate work and concluding with an ABD—All but Dissertation.

The Haggadah was my father's gesture of acceptance. By this time, he had become more of a Conservative Jew, a shift that started after our move from New York to Los Angeles when I was fourteen. Before that, my father had always been Orthodox, and my mother had always been resentful. It's like Reformed, only angrier. She didn't care who I dated, so long as I was happy. My father did care, but he knew better. Disowning me would mean divorcing my mother. That never happened.

> *Sophie and Irv go to the doctor.*
> *The examination room is divided in two with a sheet, Irv on one side and Sophie on the other.*
> *Irv shouts through the sheet, "Sophie, the doctor wants to know if we have intercourse."*
> *"If we whaaat?" Sophie shouts back.*
> *"Have intercourse!?"*
> *"No! Tell him we've got Blue Cross/Blue Shield."*

The day my mother, at home on morphine, drifted in and out of consciousness—the first of three days that ended in her death after a fourteen-year war with ovarian cancer—was the first time I ever canceled a booked performance. I was supposed to do a stand-up set at The Ice House in Pasadena, but being funny as your mother dies is a challenge I wasn't up to.

My grandmother outlived my mother. She told no jokes in those final days. She also didn't come to her daughter's funeral. She had just spent a couple of weeks visiting my mother, accompanied by my aunt and uncle, who had never been to LA before. They didn't know she would get sick the day they left, that this sickness would never resolve. She would die about a week later. No one from her side of the family returned to see her buried. My mother would have preferred to be cremated, but out of respect for my father's beliefs, she was buried at Hillside Cemetery—the final resting place of Milton Berle, Jack Benny, George Jessel, to name a few funny men. Not to mention, Al Jolson and Shelley Winters, two of my mother's favorites.

> *A family set out on a road trip but found themselves lost as the sun went down. There was nowhere to stop, so when the mother spotted a sign for a nudist colony on the side of the road, she insisted they pull in and spend the night.*
> *The next morning, they decided to wander around a little. The mother and the little boy headed out, with dad setting out a little later. Suddenly, his son runs up to him and says: "Daddy, daddy, why do some men have big ones while*

some men are very little?" The father didn't quite know what to say. Then it came to him.

"Well, my son, it's because the men with big ones are very wealthy. The little ones aren't."

The son, seemingly satisfied by the answer, ran off again—only to return about fifteen minutes later. "Daddy, Daddy." "Yes, my son?"

"There's a man talking to Mommy, and he's growing richer and richer and richer."

My mother never became a joke teller like her mother, but she did become a poet-of-sorts. After being told she had two years to live, she proved her doctors wrong. She found herself becoming a role model in her cancer support group as she kept beating the odds year after year. Among the poems she wrote was one that began:

A cancer cell is one that is defective.
That was the word I needed: I thought about it, and in my mind, it was repeated.
I knew that I could conquer a cell that was defective.
There was no question that this situation could be corrected.
When chemotherapy was prescribed, It made me feel more dead than alive.

And it ended:

*When I looked at the word che**mother**apy, I knew it would act salutarily*
And give me peace like no other,
Because there in the middle I saw the word… mother.

Jewish jokes and what one might call Jewish genius run in the family. For my grandmother, humor was a survival tool. For my mother, it was poetry. And for me? Somewhere in between. Humor and knowledge fall into the category of intangibles and, therefore, are potentially everlasting. Whereas, to quote Bret Stephens, in a New York Times OpEd, "there is the understanding, born of repeated exile, that everything that seems solid and valuable is ultimately perishable."

Knowing laughter is love, I have come to understand I was raised with plenty of both. I never did learn to tell my grandmother's jokes the way she did. But when I laugh, when I tell a story, when I let humor and life intertwine—I know I am continuing the legacy. A joyful one.

Connecting: To God
　　To Synagogue
　　　To Prayer
　　　　To The Tree of Life

Kaddish

Judy Bolton-Fasman

I Love You, My Friend

I know the word 'friend' in different languages: Cherokee—oginalii, Spanish—amigo, French—amie, Hebrew—chaver. You were once my boyfriend, but you remained my chaver for two-thirds of my life.

We swapped heart languages, you and I. I told you, 'te amo,' in Spanish, and you taught me, I love you—'Ani ohevet otha'—in your first language, Hebrew.

When we were young, we daydreamed of marrying and naming a daughter of ours Reut—the Hebrew word for deep friendship. We took words from each other's lexicons and forged our own vocabulary.

We dreamt together until we broke apart. Pieces of us scattered between Israel and America. You loved me, and you loved men too.

We stayed piecemeal—an occasional email, a birthday phone call—for over a decade until I called you out of the blue one day. What does out of the blue mean, you asked. You loved learning English expressions.

We slowly glued ourselves back together with stardust. The cracks between us glittered. Beauty and pain mingled.

When your cancer returned, you refused more chemo. I screamed at you for over an hour on the phone. Stress cracks veined our love but didn't break us this time. Two years later, as you lay dying, I secured a hard-to-find plane ticket to Israel in the middle of a war. You died on the 22nd anniversary of my father's death, mere days before I could get to you.

There is a Jewish saying that there is nothing more whole than a broken heart. To that point, I wholly love you with my broken heart.

Funeral

In your will, you were explicit about not having a funeral. For a time, my life became your funeral. It was nearly impossible in Israel to find a mortuary that would cremate you.

I had recurring nightmares of you engulfed in orange, blue-rimmed flames.

Dust to dust, the Bible commands.

Ashes, ashes we all fall down.

I almost feel your ashes between my fingers disintegrating like a dead moth's wings. Your wish, to transform yourself into a different form of matter until you are completely gone, unnerved me. You wanted to erase all traces of you in this world. But know, 'chaver sheli,' my friend, your erasure has backfired because everything concerning you has become a shrine—a photograph of us together, a saved voicemail, a text message in which you asked forgiveness for a slight only you noticed.

Etz Chaim—Tree of Life

Always a tree of life—dead trees still nourish younger living ones. That's not so different from our dead nourishing us one way or another. The stump connects to one or more of the trees around it, usually through its roots. Water flowing through a full-size tree directs water and life to the stump. That stump will never green again, make cones, seeds, or pollen, or lay claim again to its towering verticality. But at least for the moment, it won't die. And who is to say it won't live forever?

Underground, trees are intimately connected. The fungi on their roots can wire adjacent trees to one another and ferry nutrients between them, creating what ecologists call a "wood-wide web." The roots themselves can also graft directly onto one another—a phenomenon documented in more than one hundred species of trees but still mysterious.

Another shrine for you: our own wood-wide web.

Mourner's Kaddish

There is not a single word about death in the Mourner's Kaddish—just praise for an unnamed God and the suggestion of posterity. This life-and-death relationship is symbiotic, like the dead trees nourishing the living ones. Ahava, *love*. Reut, deep friendship. Reut, our imaginary daughter, whose free-floating soul will find yours.

My Akedah

Tzivia Gover

I whispered my daughter awake before dawn.

Her hair was a wispy cloud, storm-tousled by dreams. She lifted her eyes and interrogated the charcoal sky that blotted the window black. "Why are we waking up in the dark?" she asked.

I don't remember exactly what I told her, except that it was a lie.

Just as what Abraham told Isaac, when the boy asked about the lamb for the sacrifice, was a lie, too.

I helped her wash and dress. Then we shambled into the car and to an all-night diner where we smothered our pancakes in watery maple syrup.

She wanted to know why we were eating breakfast out instead of filling bowls with cereal and milk at home.

What fairytale version of the grim truth could I feed her?

A nightmare phone call: My ex, my daughter's other mother, saying she was getting in the car, was on her way. Detailing the harm she'd do to me, to our house. Then a call from the local sheriff accusing me of kidnapping my own child.

I did the math. She'd be arriving at our empty house just about now, as dawn was spilling its yolk-orange sunshine over the diner's asphalt parking lot.

After breakfast I said goodbye to my daughter at the door of our friend's home. Then I drove to court, not knowing that I would come back down the mountain alone.

§

When the midwife guided her from my partner's body, our daughter's eyes opened wide in the fluorescent-lit wonder she'd been born into.

She was always eager and expectant like that. Grabbed fistfuls of bread well before we were advised to feed her solid foods. Was so insistent that we relented, with offerings of pizza and bits of bagels she'd gum away at.

She was talking before she knew any words. We scribed a lexicon of her expressive babbles. Named each one: Baby Eating Elephant, or Goat Tangled in Hose.

Her chin was perpetually tipped upward, and her mouth opened wide with peals of delight. She loved being lifted toward the sky and being pushed into dizzying arcs on the swing. The watchword of her faith was, *More, more! Higher, higher!*

My partner filled canvases with bright distortions, tested the limits of truth, and expressed her emotions in sudden and dramatic outbursts. I convinced myself that her eccentricities were signs of her artistic temperament and that our love could calm her careening swings between effusive generosity and ferocious silences.

I underestimated the hellfire of the gods of bipolar and borderline. I didn't know the prayers to repeat in the Temples of Diagnosis.

Didn't know that our first embrace was a covenant, and that though we could not keep it, it would keep its grip on us.

We blamed. We stormed. We held on.

We maintained. We managed.

We separated. We shared custody.

In the beginning.

Then, when our daughter was four, my ex moved with her out of state. This attempt at a geographic cure was no remedy. Her mind was desert and prophet. Was a wilderness to be crossed with sirens blaring and blue lights flashing. Dwelled in emergency rooms in the country of bandaged wrists.

She in treatment. Me with my daughter. For a few weeks? A few months? "Until you are healthy again," I told my ex.

And when she said, "Yes, I'm ready." I said, "No."

She was not.

In this beginning, gay marriage was a rainbow-misted dream, and children were being taken from their lesbian parents as a matter of course.

The judge gaveled my motherhood away. Declared me a Biological Stranger to my child. Forbade contact between us. Not in person. Not by phone. Not by mail. Not at all.

As they climbed Mount Moriah, Abraham and Isaac were accompanied by servants. But for the final leg of their three-day journey, they walked alone.

For years I climbed my mountain of anger and grief. I was loved by a new partner, my family, and friends. But I was also alone. A daughterless mother.

A ram caught in a thicket and the voice of an angel spared Abraham his murderous burden.

"I can't imagine," friends and not-friends told me. "*I* wouldn't be able to bear it," they said.

I bore what I had to bear.

Until nearly five years had passed. And I rose in the pitch-dark belly of a late-winter night in that hourless hour when the face of the clock is washed clean. Inexplicably, the tumult in my head lifted, and I melted into a bright peace. Half-dreaming, I descended the stairs from my bedroom. Barefoot and robed like a ghost, or a goddess, I stood in the living room.

Hineini, I said. *I am here.*

I placed a photograph of my daughter wearing a princess dress and a headband that she wore like a tiara. I lit a tea candle and bounded these objects with strings of Mardi Gras beads.

I consecrated the moment with an unscripted prayer.

Take my child. My only child. The one I love.

I delivered her into the unseen hands of the One. One, who is greater than anything in the DSM. Greater than the social workers, and the fractured wills of me and my ex. Greater than the lawyers and the laws and the judges and the wood-paneled temples of Who Can and Who Cannot.

I bundled my grievances against God like a sheaf of ribbon-bound letters from a long-ago affair. I fed them, one by one, into the flame.

My faith broke free from the tangled thicket and rose up like smoky incense.

And I made peace with the god who I thought had hardened his heart to my years-long howl of protest and grief.

Before that night all I knew was a story that lived in a scroll—

A story that I read once a year in synagogue—

Abraham and Isaac on the mountain with kindling and knife—

The crust of that cruel tale shattered like crystal beneath my heel. Out from the shards came the truth that lives in myth.

And now:

Me at the altar with matchbook and flame—

Me at the page, with an alphabet of grace—

Writing *Surrender* across every page.

I didn't know then that El Shaddai was the name of the One who promised Abraham and Sarah a child. She whose name means The Many Breasted One. The All Sufficient One. The One Who Provides. I didn't know that She presides over the mountains and high places.

That night, in my cottage perched on a rise the locals call Bear Mountain, the deity whose name I did not yet know, shushed me in Her arms and cradled my faraway daughter, too.

This was the god of life and death, of source and substance. This was a mother as fierce as I was.

She said, *Let go. Love.*

You must let go, Love.

This was my Akedah.

I came down from my mountain.

And I climbed back up to my bed.

I slipped beneath the blankets and, at last, I lay down to rest.

Just weeks after my fight had burned to ash, the call came. Not ram, not angel—but a ringing phone. I lifted the receiver and heard my daughter's bright voice: *Ima!* she cried.

Before the month cycled to a close, she was in my arms again.
Who was Isaac when he came down the mountain?
I didn't know to ask that question.

And what about Ishmael? And Hagar? And what about Sarah?

§

I once read an account of a mother whose child had been kidnapped. And years later was returned. The joy of reunion was also furious heartbreak.
The captor is the captor. Time, indifferent, is the relentless enemy.

While she was gone her cells multiplied. Grew. Gained. Shed themselves.
And she grew some more.
Bones broke and were healed.
And I was ignorant of all of it.
Isaac wandered back down the mountain alone. When he reached his mother's house it had been days, not years. He weighed not one ounce more. Amassed no new firmness of muscle. There would have been bruises, but nothing to match the storm-purple chaos blossoming inside him.
His laugh would return.
But with a hint of terror in it.

§

My daughter and I, we staggered forth, stunned and scorched, into our lives.
Decades have passed. We have grown, broken and healed what we can. We honor what the other can never say. Recognize rage that crawls on all fours. Know the heart's fierce beauty as we never dreamed we'd need to.
Our text messages to one another end in strings of emoji-glyphs in countless patterns. As if some catenation of rainbows and dancing hearts could release what is trapped inside our losses.

Only a small subset of mothers will know what I'm talking about.
Only now do I realize that Sarah would have been among them.

My Father's Blessings, My Mother's Stones: A D'var Torah*

Jena Schwartz

Encountering Torah can feel like standing at the threshold of the ocean: vast and overwhelming, much like life itself. I find it helpful to pause before diving in, to feel the sand beneath us, the temperature of the water lapping over our feet. We might take in the wide horizon and feel awe—a little fear, a little wonder—at all these depths contain, most of which we will never see. Then, we can step forward, appreciating how amazing it is to experience even an inlet of these waters.

This is how I invite us to enter *Parshat Vayetze*: slowly and mindfully. It may have oceanic potential and infinite meaning, but as with anything, we can only begin to understand it by choosing one focal point.

As with any *parsha*, there is the visible story and, as with the ocean, the intricate ecosystems beneath the surface. I hope this *d'var* will result in something tangible to hold, as if bringing a shell or a stone with us from the shore.

§

Veyetze opens with Jacob setting out on his journey from Beer-Sheva and stopping to rest for a night. He takes a stone for a pillow, which doesn't sound very comfortable, but, one imagines, he's making do with what is available to him.

He dreams his now-famous dream about the ladder with messengers going up and down from Heaven, and the intergenerational blessing of home and abundance he receives from Adonai. Not only does God tell Jacob: אֲנִי יְהוָה אֱלֹהֵי אַבְרָהָם אָבִיךָ—*I am the God of your father Abraham's house*—but, according to *Chizkuni*, the commentaries of Rabbi Hezekiah ben Manoah, the very stone Jacob used as a pillow and later anointed with oil "had been part of the altar on which his father Yitzchok had been bound on the occasion of the Akeydah."

Even before he begins to dream, Jacob is already subconsciously linking the stories between past and future generations.

I question the word "IF" in Jacob's acceptance of God's unconditional blessing; his vow to Adonai implies that he doesn't fully trust God to follow through: "**If** God remains with me, protecting me on this journey that I am making, and giving me bread to eat and clothing to wear, and I return safe to my father's house— יהוה shall be my God."

Despite Jacob's uncertainty, he anoints the stone with oil and renames the place where he slept Bethel, House of God. What can we make of this?

§

The thing with dreams is that they're ethereal. They may leave us with a promise, or even a vision of something so much bigger than ourselves, it's ungraspable.

Jacob wakes up "shaken" by the dream. He seems genuinely surprised that he hadn't known before that God was in this place. *Ma nora ha makom ha ze*, he exclaims. How awesome is this place! But he does something else— he pours oil on the very stone that was present on that fateful day for his father.

Though Jacob leaves Bethel that day, the stone remains a marker of memory and a physical embodiment of God's blessing. I wonder if it also represents something else: An obligation.

§

As I pondered the many possible meanings of this story, I found myself thinking about the bag of stones I'd been driving around with for months.

Yes, I've been driving around since this summer with a Ziplock bag of rocks in the trunk of my hybrid Corolla. More than once, I've thought, *I've got to write about this!* There was something slightly absurd about it, yet I sensed a deeper meaning there.

When I encountered this *parsha*, suddenly I began to see why I've been holding onto these stones. For one thing, I told my mom I would, and that is reason enough. You should know that I collected the stones from the porch of my parents' home of forty years, which they recently sold.

Starting at age ten, this was where I had many dreams, literal and figurative, about what blessings life might hold. Finding my way forth required much wandering, sometimes through fear itself. My path, like all our paths, required faith. There were many years when I felt I was swimming in a vast ocean of becoming, with nothing to hold onto, not even a physical place to which I would return.

What I did have—and what this story helps me see—was the blessing of my parents' enduring love and support.

When it came time earlier this year to help them prepare to leave this home, my mom asked, "What about my rocks?" Her question did not surprise me, as she was very attached to the stones she placed around the edges of the side porch and the old Victorian barn. I knew leaving this place held grief and uncertainty for her.

I said, "Mom, don't worry, we'll take these rocks and find a new home for them."

"I've got an even better idea," she said, suggesting that we bring the stones to the plots at the Wildwood Cemetery, where she and my dad will eventually be buried. Suddenly, the stones had the potential to link past and future, becoming symbols of the connections between Jacob's dream and the very descendants God promised him.

§

Hamakom, the word meaning "the place" that appears five times in *Vayetze*, has become one of the many names for God. This *parsha* shows us that the place may not be a physical one. God travels with us, and stones become markers of life-affirming dreams across generations. The place is both literal—Bethel—and figurative—wherever we rest our heads and dream.

Stones provide a way to take that which is too vast for us to comprehend and make it manifest. Sometimes we find ourselves driving around town with rocks in the trunks of our cars, reminding us to have faith even when we're not at all sure where the journey is taking us, and even if we wonder whether God will follow through on God's promise at all.

The 20th century French philosopher Jacques Derrida wrote, "Inheritance is never a *given*, it is always a task." Even though God blessed Jacob freely and unconditionally, Jacob's task still lay before him: To become Israel. Many more chapters await him on that journey. But anointing the stone is an important step toward his becoming himself and fully receiving God's blessing. It is not enough to sleep and dream and be blessed. We must wake up and take action.

The stone as a marker of *hamakom* is much bigger than the place itself. It is a powerful way of linking each generation to the ones before and those yet to come. The same is true for shepherding my mother's stones from her beloved home to her eventual grave. Likewise, trusting my own creative and spiritual path is my own journey of receiving and fulfilling God's blessing and becoming fully myself.

I think of a different story about another famous stone, the one Sisyphus was condemned to push up a mountain for all his days. To see life in this way is to betray God's blessing. Instead, I look to Jacob's story as an affirmation of God's presence and the task of this vast inheritance that calls us to wake up where we are and see that God is here.

When I feel doubt alongside my gratitude for being alive, when blessings feel as ethereal and fleeting as dreams, I often turn to poetry. This week, I found comfort and renewal in the opening lines of Doris L. Ferleger's 2024 poem, "Stone for a Pillow":

> *Dear God of Abandoned Hope,*
> *I entreat You, may I feel each stone You place*
> *under my head as a bolster of bright brocade.*

May we rest and dream, may we journey bravely into the unknown, and may we wake up each morning knowing that the stones we sleep on and the ones we anoint as holy are interchangeable with invocations of God's promise and presence.

May we return to hope every time we place a stone on a loved one's grave or pick one up from the ocean floor. Ours is not a journey for the wary, yet we are blessed to continue it. *Hamakom* is right here, among us, with the stones that mark it so.

---

* Literally "a word of Torah" in Hebrew, a *d'var* explores and draws meaning from the week's *parsha*, or Torah portion. It should engage with the text in ways that offer us something pertinent to consider, pose questions to ponder, and/or open new possibilities for understanding and relating to ourselves, each other, Judaism, and the world.

The Old Shul

Ellen Levitt

We Jews have so many types of traditions and means of honoring our connections. These come in a myriad of forms: from praying to cooking and baking, music and arts, from lighting candles to reciting blessings, to dancing and humor and more. We revisit old customs and create new ones. There are many common and comforting traditions with which we engage, especially when it comes to holidays and life's milestones. But we also have our individual shtick, to put it frankly. Most Jewish folks I know do have their particular traditions upon which they put their individualistic stamp. Some have been handed down from generation to generation and others may only last for the duration of one person's lifetime.

I have a certain way of honoring tradition and cultivating connection to the past. It's by documenting Lost Synagogues.

I am fascinated by—really, obsessed with—former synagogues and other Jewish institutional buildings. I have been visiting, photographing, and researching these sites since 1999, when on my birthday, I drove around the neighborhood of my earliest years, spent in Flatbush, Brooklyn, to shoot black-and-white photographs of the area. During this photo session I came upon two former synagogues: one was my first shul and the other was my mother's childhood shul. Both had since been turned into churches.

Since that fateful day in April 1999, I have visited a few hundred such sites throughout New York City, and a few hundred more within New York State, New Jersey, Connecticut, and Pennsylvania. I've scoured cities such as Chicago, Detroit, Seattle, Cleveland, Baltimore and elsewhere, in search of one-time synagogues. They vary in size and condition; some retain a great deal of Judaica while others have barely any. Some are gorgeous while others are utilitarian or even dumpy. A large percentage are now churches, but others are used as schools, private homes, medical facilities, art galleries, and so on. A handful I've come across were abandoned.

I have revisited many throughout New York City on more than one occasion, to see how they have fared, noting changes and stability, and partly because I feel a connection to them. Their presence means a lot to me: while documenting them I have written three books (with another in the works) and several articles. I have maintained two Facebook pages (although the original was subjected to an antisemitic hack) and have created exhibitions based upon the photographs I have taken.

The synagogue I have revisited most frequently is that very first one, which was the second home—and the only remaining one standing—of Shaare Torah. I went to Shaare Torah with my family until I was not quite seven years old, and I have definite memories of the place. I would go to prayer services with my father and imitate whatever the other congregants did. I remember the red carpet in the main sanctuary. I had such fun when I was five or six, on Simchat Torah, dressed up fancy, grasping a paper flag, and dancing around on the street in front of the synagogue.

One time around 2009 or 2010, Dad and I accompanied a man named Charles who interviewed us in the former synagogue, now a Baptist Church, while another man filmed us. It was humbling and fascinating to see how the interior of the old Shaare Torah had been kept similar in certain ways but changed in others. For instance, the doors that had been on the Holy Ark had been moved to the Choir Loft, but that red carpet I recalled fondly was still there.

Shaare Torah closed in the late 1970s and members merged into two other Brooklyn synagogues. I attend one of those, Flatbush Jewish Center, and one of our senior congregants, Mike, who came over from Shaare Torah, is my link to our former shul. He gave me a photocopied image of the original Shaare Torah building, which is long gone. (It was knocked down and an elementary school was built on the plot.)

I studied that picture, and then, with a jolt of regret, realized I had seen that building several times as a child and young adult! I had driven past it with my parents, who had referred to it as a "haunted house." They never told me it had been the older Shaare Torah. Had I known, I would have taken photographs of it, even in its decrepit condition.

I cannot go back in time and bring back that old building, but I do revisit the Shaare Torah I knew, pondering my childhood memories, and admiring the unusual decorative elements of the building, from the Ludwig Wolpert designed sculpture-sign, to the menorahs on the banisters. By paying homage to Shaare Torah in person, I give credit to the place for being the catalyst of my Lost Synagogues exploration and part-time career in writing, photography, and leading tours.

Shaare Torah is now Salem Missionary Baptist Church. I realize some people are saddened by that fact. Some people are uncomfortable with my work and think of it as showing the failures of Jewish people to hold onto their old shuls. But I see it differently. The vast majority of these old shuls, including Shaare Torah, were vacated voluntarily, if with remorse and regrets. It is better to remember these synagogues and document what remains than to ignore their presence. To me, visiting Shaare Torah is a semi-regular ritual that connects me in various manners to my past as well as my present.

I wouldn't say this is a happy ritual, but it isn't mournful. Stopping by is a mix of nostalgia and jogging my memory, honoring the place that inspired my scholarly work, but also something I cannot quite explain. I feel drawn to the synagogue. Shaare Torah is important to me in clear ways as well as for elusive reasons. And that, to some extent, is how I view Judaism: very familiar yet, at times, difficult to explain. That's fine. You don't have to be able to reason with everything. There is power and beauty in mystery.

That Temple Feeling*
Ronit Plank

About three months before my daughter's Bat Mitzvah, we go to Israel and our guide for the ten days corrects us when we use the word "temple" to refer to our reform synagogue. He says in Israel temple means the old Temple, the Temple-temple where Jews slide notes into worn stone. He tells us we should call where we go in Seattle for Friday night services and High Holy Days a synagogue. We return from our trip careful to say synagogue but gradually forget.

My first temple is the Free Synagogue of Flushing in Queens which we join the year after my mother leaves me and my younger sister with our father. The majestic domed building sits atop a respectable number of steps on the corner of Kissena Blvd and Sanford Avenue, four Corinthian columns completing its neoclassical look. Inside, rows and rows of dark brown wood pews fill the sanctuary, bordered on either side by intricate stained-glass windows. The bimah's rich red carpet will soften our footsteps when in several years' time my sister and I are called to the Torah; blush-plum marble surrounds the ark which is protected by sleek gold doors. The building speaks of history and permanence in ways that soothe me. Each Friday a lush bouquet of fresh flowers adorns the lectern from which our sometimes-irascible rabbi delivers the sermon and our tall, bald cantor's bass-baritone thunders through the air. During Shabbat services I gaze at the multi-colored windows surrounding me and try to count the endless sections of gold-and-orange-stained glass that form the Magen David in the dome's peak, gold and orange glass rays beaming over our heads.

You need to be around other Jews, my father says, when we complain about having to attend religious school for two extra hours of class time twice a week. My sister and I meet up after our regular P.S. 20 school day to walk the five blocks to the Free Synagogue. Even when I kvetch about the dark and cold during winter, about missing out on daylight and sweet warming weather in spring, about not having time to do regular-school homework, about how dorky I feel going to Hebrew school, my father says we must.

Israeli dancing and singing Hebrew songs with the rabbi's daughter are the best parts of Hebrew school for me. She mimeographs song sheets for us, helps us roll out dough for Hamantaschen, and shows us how to braid challah. What is it like, I wonder, to work for your father, to be in this building so many days a week, to feel so Jewish all the time.

Spanish Jews, Ethiopian Jews, Indian Jews—we learn that all around the world there are Jews like us reciting prayers, getting B'nai Mitzvah'd. The rabbi's wife teaches me how to read Hebrew in third grade, and once I understand the vowels I am off and running. In fourth grade I have a crush on Mr. Stein, tall and handsome enough for a Hebrew school teacher; I smart-alleck him the way I do sometimes with my father and feel pretty in my flowered dress. In fifth grade I have a teacher whose son has a crush on me and who I think is pretty okay for Hebrew school but would not flirt with in regular school.

Right after services on Friday nights we go downstairs for Oneg Shabbat. White plastic tablecloths cover large round tables, platters of rugelach, babka, and danish laid out on each one. The room smells of freshly brewed, slightly burnt coffee and floral perfumes. Looking for my friends, I grab a few pieces of pastry we never get at home and rush past the old women gathering, a sea of white, gray, and orange hair-sprayed heads, coral and red lipsticks staining the rims of their mugs. They sit hunched in metal chairs, their necks bent in inelegant ways, chatting and watching the room, these women who lived through the war, who might have experienced the Holocaust firsthand—I never ask. I want to rush past them, even when one compliments my patent leather Mary Janes. Thank you, I say, registering veined and wrinkled hands and the opportunity I have to stay a moment and be kinder, but I keep moving. I don't yet understand how a room beats with history and what's been lost. All I know as I dart away is that I don't want to ever be like them. I don't realize this place has already seeped into me.

After my Bat Mitzvah I go to temple less and less. The Free Synagogue holds a confirmation service for me and a handful of us teens. Confirmation means I can stop spending Friday nights there, practicing Hebrew, being part of a community. I've looked forward to the chance to leave since we first joined. When my father marries my stepmom, we move to Long Island and don't go back to Flushing ever again. My family and I are accustomed to saying goodbye to places without worrying what we'll have left.

Each of my best college friends has partnered off by the time I'm 26 and, hoping to marry a Jew, I join JDate but only manage a few dates on the east and then the west coast. The several guys I meet up with don't seem impressed with me and I'm not impressed with them. When my raised-Catholic-but-lapsed husband and I get serious, I tell him our children will be Bat or Bar Mitzvah'd but not baptized. That doesn't seem fair, he says. Well, that's how it must be, I say, and worry he'll end it. But I also feel brave. I've made my Jewishness worth fighting for.

Looking for community we join a Seattle temple when my daughter is four and my son two. I teach Hebrew reading and writing to 3rd graders, Holocaust history to 7th graders, and electives like Jewish Yoga for 8th graders. When I take my third-grade class to Sunday kids' services I make sure they are settled and safe and then I look out for my own children. My daughter's eyes find mine and I smile, my son waves, and I sit as proud as a puffed-up mother hen. The inside of this temple is different from the Free Synagogue, not what I'm used to, not nearly pretty enough, but nice in its own way, giant windows surrounding us. All of us sit tucked in sanctuary seats, thick beams of wood arcing above our heads, slicing up the gray Pacific Northwest sky.

Clearing the table I hear my husband belting the Sh'ma from the living room in his warm tenor voice while our oldest dog stares at him and wags his tail. My goyishe husband loves my Jewishness and he tosses out words like schmuck, meshugas, and yenta as if he grew up with them. I think about how if I'd wanted to have super Jewish kids I could have held the line in my late twenties and only dated Jewish men. I think about what teaching your children Jewishness means if they ultimately don't practice it.

How do I know if my children will remember—have it in their bodies, in their bones—that temple feeling? Do all the years at religious school and preparing for a Bnai Mitzvah matter if they no longer know the prayers by heart, don't go to temple, don't marry a Jew?

And then I think about how my Judaism is anchored in my parents' cultural Jewishness, in our family story. My children laugh with my mother whose Brooklyn accent seems to get stronger every year, and at twenty and eighteen they still search alongside their younger cousins for the Afikomen my father hides. Maybe they will recall Shabbat nights at home, me lighting the candles; maybe they'll carry this family feeling, this Jewish feeling with them. So much is going to be gone one day; I hope my children hold onto a little of what I have left them.

I return to Flushing with my husband and kids in 2016, the first time I've been back since leaving at fifteen. When we get to the corner of Kissena Boulevard and Sanford Avenue and I see the steps leading up to the temple, my breath catches. Those classrooms and the social hall where I spent afternoons and evenings singing Hebrew songs and dancing the Hora with my other reluctant friends was where I belonged, and the watchful old women I rushed past every Shabbat, my extended family. My father was right, I needed those Jews. Growing up I didn't think of the synagogue as home, but it was. That time is over, those women are gone now, but I can still see them in their chairs watching me and my classmates chasing each other and laughing. If I could go back, if they were still here, I would stop when they spoke to me, I would ask to sit at their table, I would listen. I didn't know then that you can miss what you once longed to escape.

---

*I used the acronym for Am Yisrael Chai as the anchoring structure for "That Temple Feeling" because I can't remember a time when I didn't know how vital those three words together are for the Jewish people. Before I had any words for this essay, I knew Am Yisrael Chai needed to be there in this way.

Light in the Empty Sanctuary
Gabrielle Ariella Kaplan-Mayer

"I'll see you after rehearsal," Mom says, as I hop out of the station wagon and walk towards the temple's back door.

I panic for a moment, thinking I might have left my practice paper in the car. But it's right here, right in my coat packet where I put it, folded up into a little square. I've read from this paper a million or more times. I've highlighted it with my sweet-scented rainbow markers. I've left it in my Trapper Keeper so I can look over my Torah portion during study hall. I've put it back together with tiny pieces of scotch tape every time the paper rips.

I'm relieved I have it with me, but it only serves as insurance. Today, I will put this paper down and read from the actual Torah scroll.

I run through the temple hallway to find Rabbi Stein. "Hello Gab!" he calls from his office door. "Ready to go?"

We walk into the sanctuary together. It's … empty. I've never been in an empty sanctuary before. I look into the pews, the ones where I've sat for hundreds of Friday nights with my family, singing Shabbat prayers. I picture myself leaning up to whisper to my best friend Joellyn whose family sits right in front of us. We've mastered how to be just loud enough to hear each other, but quiet enough not to get yelled at.

With no one in the sanctuary, it feels kind of … lonely.

Rabbi Stein walks up to the bima. He takes the Torah scroll from the ark. "We're going to undress the Torah verrrrryyyy carefully," he says. "You take the *rimonim* off, lay them on the table." We work together in a nice rhythm: first I remove the silver crowns, then the breast plate (so awkward) and last the pointer. Rabbi Stein sits back in one of the bima chairs where you get to sit if you're a reader. He cradles the Torah while I remove its purple velvet cover.

"Okay, kiddo, here we go," he says. "Show time!"

He lays the Torah on the reading table, and we roll it forward to my portion. He takes the silver *yad* and quickly locates my first letter. It's a *vav*. I peer into the scroll. "*V'yidabar Adonai el Moshe lamore*," I begin. It's not so hard without the vowels. I can do this.

"You know your stuff," Rabbi Stein says. "Go ahead, don't worry if you stumble. We will practice a few times."

We? He means me. It's me who's going to be standing up here in a few days, in front of my out-of-town family and family friends, the friends I invited from school, and all of the old ladies who serve tea at Friday night *Onegs* and yell at Joellyn and me for stealing all of the lemons and dipping them into sugar. "Girls, who do you think slices those lemons?" Mrs. Kramer asks, her eyes peering down over her glasses like daggers.

Why did I invite anyone from school?

Barbara, the temple's secretary, appears before us, interrupting my thoughts: "Rabbi, you're needed on an urgent call." The look on her face says it all. Everyone knows Barbara runs this place.

"Keep reading, Gab," Rabbi Stein calls, hurrying out the sanctuary side door. "Read it a few times. Be right back!"

He's gone. I'm all alone with a Torah open in front of me. The sanctuary is really, really quiet. I could just go wait in the bathroom. But I guess I should practice. I stay.

I pick up the *yad* and look for the *vav* again. It's really pretty, how the letters are written on the scroll in black ink. Rabbi Stein showed us a video about that, how a scribe sits and writes the letters, dipping a calligraphy pen in ink.

Once I find the *vav*, it seems to skip around: I imagine it dancing, teasing me a little. I chase one letter, then another. My nerves melt away. I know my portion. This is not a big deal.

Afternoon sunlight streams in through the tall windows made of purple, blue, red, and yellow stained-glass. They are models of Marc Chagall's windows in Jerusalem, Mom told me. I love to stare at the windows during services. Some of them have animals on them. The windows look different today, though, like the light is coming through them in a more intense way.

I start to read out loud, from the top. The letters jump out of the scroll, landing in my voice. My voice calls out the ancient Hebrew words to the empty sanctuary. The *yad* in my hand feels electric—is it supposed to feel that way?

I make it to the end of my portion, stumbling only a couple of times. I pause for a second to take a breath and glance up from the scroll. The light seems to be hanging in the air now. It is dense and present, like it has its own life.

I stay quiet with the light, feeling it. Maybe I am actually not alone. Maybe the light is God?

I have no idea how long Rabbi Stein has been gone or how long I've been standing here. It could be a minute; it could be a day.

I start over, read again. But this time, I read *to* the light. I look up from time to time and the light is still there. The light seems happy, as if it really likes hearing me read from the Torah. I don't make any mistakes.

"Do you want to hear it again?" I ask, having no idea whom I'm speaking to.

I start again, one more time. The sanctuary feels full now. It feels like *love*. It feels like everything is going to be okay.

Rabbi Stein comes rushing back, a little sweaty. "I'm sorry to leave you like that, Gab," he says. "Go ahead and read again so I can make sure your voice carries." He sits down in a pew near the very back.

I begin to read in a loud voice. The light through the windows shifts. It gets dark. It's back to just Rabbi Stein and me in the sanctuary again.

"Very good," he says, when I finish. "Very good." He walks up to the bima, and we roll the Torah scroll, put on its velvet cover and crowns, and return it to the ark. *Goodbye letters,* I think, *see you on the big day.*

Mom comes to pick me up. We have to stop and get my Bat Mitzvah dress from the seamstress. Mom puts on the radio in the car and hands me Ritz crackers to snack on. Cyndi Lauper sings *Girls Just Wanna Have Fun*.

"How was the rehearsal?" Mom asks.

I know Mom says the *shema* every night before bed and asks God to bless us, but we have never spoken about what God *feels* like, if she's ever felt that presence. It will take years before I find the words or begin to understand what that light may have been.

So I keep what happened in the sanctuary been the light and me.

"Fine," I say. "It was fine."

Kaddish Confessions

Megan Vered

The Mourner's Kaddish grabbed me by the kishkas when I was thirteen, when death first left its footprint on my life. My grandmother had been hit by a car when crossing a Los Angeles street, and my friend Ann's older brother, too young, had been killed in a jeep accident. These collisions with finality led to funerals and burials and evenings of sitting shiva, where huddles of people swathed in black mumbled incomprehensible, seemingly morbid words.

That summer at camp, in solidarity with Ann's grief, my friend Steph and I, in the way of teenage girls who make tacit agreements without having to utter a word, took on the Kaddish prayer with a sense of mission. We recited the compressed succession of words during outdoor services, beneath the halo of scented redwoods. Like toddlers acquiring language, we repeated the phrases while wandering paths of pine needles, the heavy stone of mourning grounding us to the earth. The prayer felt clumsy in my mouth. I was relieved every time we hit the final v'im'ru: amen.

I knew the Kaddish was a memorial prayer. I didn't know what the words meant. I knew that we stood while saying it. I didn't know that Kaddish meant sanctification in Aramaic. I knew it held great meaning, particularly for the elders in our congregation. I didn't know how difficult it would be to commit the words to memory.

By the final Shabbat service—all of us dressed in white—Steph had mastered the prayer while I, who was no slouch when it came to language memorization, continued to fumble the multi-syllabic flow. Steph never knew I was faking it because I launched the opening with assurance: Yitgadal v'yitkadash sh'mei raba.

By the time I faltered, my voice had become a tiny thread in the group intonation. Nobody noticed. Why did this prayer challenge me? Was it my fear of death? The solemn tone? The Aramaic words? Whatever the reason, I could not make it stick. On the bus ride home, duffels packed with dusty, sun worn clothing, I bounced on my bench seat singing spirited Hebrew songs, every word clean and crisp

The truth is the Kaddish prayer scared me. Death and funerals scared me. Sunday school Holocaust movies scared me. I didn't understand why anyone would willingly attend an event centered around a dead person, was unable to grasp the value of collective grief, and flinched at the gloom that seized the synagogue when names of the dead were recited, followed by the dirge-like prayer. I was a *l'chaim* Jew through and through.

I didn't know then that the Kaddish was anything but somber. I never would have guessed from the heavy tone of lament that it was a glorious, high-praise contemplation about the light of the divine, the sanctity of heaven, and the hope for eternal peace—one of the most elevated prayers in the Jewish service.

I now understand that the prayer, which begins with the words, *May God's great name be exalted and sanctifies, throughout the world, which God has created, according to plan,* is meant to bring comfort and purpose to those who remain. It elevates us from suffering and the limitations of mortality, bringing us closer to the divine, in whatever form that takes.

For years I continued my swindle as a Kaddish imposter. In the excruciating days following October 7, my brother Oran called to tell me he had a dream in which his rabbi gave him the sacred task of helping the souls of those who had been murdered ascend to heaven. My brother, honored to be granted this virtuous assignment, began a special prayer practice to bring light and ease to those who had so brutally lost their lives.

After we hung up, I thought, if my brother is guiding souls to heaven, the least I can do is recite the Kaddish in their honor. I remembered a small white index card I'd received at the recent funeral of our long-time family rabbi, who had officiated my first wedding as well as my grandparents' and parents' funerals. The words of the Kaddish were printed on it. I placed it on my desk, repeating the words again and again, invoking the long-ago hum of summer redwoods.

I downloaded a version onto my phone, listened to it in the car, and became a regular at Shabbat services for the first time in my life, where I recited the words in earnest. I typed up a cheat sheet, changing the font for the English translation to red. Still, I felt outwitted by the words, unable to lift them off the page in particular the second stanza in which a string of words that began with "y" stuck together like gluey porridge in my mouth, words that when translated formed a different kind of glue, one that binds us to the divine: *Blessed, praised, honored, exalted, extolled, glorified, adored, and lauded be the name of the Holy Blessed One, beyond all earthly words and songs of blessing, praise, and comfort.*

I believed if I could commit the glory of this prayer to heart, I could be part of the healing effort. Then, it clicked—memorization was not the aspiration. I was not being judged, nor would I ever be expected to deliver a solo performance given that the Kaddish can only be recited with a minimum quorum of ten adult Jews. Above that, as Steph recently said, "We are all imperfect, but as a group we create something resembling wholeness." Maybe this one imperfect prayer was my personal arrangement with the divine that had no bearing on my worth as a Jew, a person, or a mourner. It was my Kaddish.

I may never have the zitsfleysh to commit this prayer to memory. It may remain beyond my grasp, one of many heights I am unable to clear in this lifetime. Yet my struggle with the words has taught me there are no flaws when remembering those who have passed.

The Understory

Jennifer Fliss

What is a tree, to a Jew?

We plant trees in a land where many of us have never been. The bushy tree of life is evident in more than one synagogue's stained-glass window. We have an entire holiday, Tu B'shevat, celebrating trees. *Bal tashchit,* while it also now applies to other things, began as an order against the destruction of trees and is a guiding principle of Jewish ethics.

Is there a more fitting place for humans to atone on Yom Kippur than in a grove of redwoods? Where, right now in the Presidio, the city is planting new trees in an attempt at reforestation. Is there a more apt metaphor for Jews in this world? Cut down by the masses, and steadily, slowly, trying to rebuild ourselves, our community?

For the oxygen. For the protection. For the network of roots and breath connecting us all.

My ten-year-old daughter and I are in San Francisco visiting R, a friend whom I've known for nearly twenty years. A lifetime. Someone's lifetime. We met in Israel during the emotional vortex of a Birthright trip.

This year on this holy day, we find ourselves in the Presidio, in a copse of redwood trees. The local synagogue has planned a meditation service for the contemplative holiday in the protective embrace of nature.

Under the tree canopy, we sit on the blanket of one of R's friends. There are, surprisingly, seven of us spread on M's blankets, sharing the space, tucked in tightly beside each other. I can't really see the rabbi or the team running the service, as there is a redwood directly in front of me, but my view isn't entirely obstructed; the tree has split into two, and in the V, I see the occasional flip of a tallit, or an arm strumming a guitar. Otherwise, my view is the striated worn bark of a massive redwood.

My daughter rests her head on my thigh; I run my fingers through her hair. Beside her is R, who occasionally reaches over to touch my arm, smile in that way she smiles, lets me know how special it is that I am there. That we are there. That we are all there sharing this communal, ethereal, arboreal experience together. We Jews here are the understory.

Redwoods have a dense root system that spreads far and wide, tangling with that of other redwoods for added stability. These trees also have high tannin levels. That means that no resin or pitch spills from its bark, and they are relatively immune to fungi, insects, and other tree diseases. Miraculously, they are also quite resistant to fire, of which there have been plenty plaguing forests throughout the American West. These trees. They just keep on surviving.

Redwoods aren't completely indestructible, though. The logging industry—also known simply, as "humans"—decimated forests throughout the country. Attempts at reforestation have met mixed results. But in addition to the saplings in this urban forest and others, there are still ancient trees, forests left to grow, flourish. People travel on vacations to take photos with the largest of them, trying to stretch their arms around the width, unable to do so. One cannot hold it all in one hand, or one armful. They are boundless.

It is Fleet Week in San Francisco. There are fighter jet demonstrations all weekend. Above the far, far away treetops, I glimpse a jet, careening its way through the sky, deafening, sonic. The rabbi laughs when he is interrupted by the noise while sharing a poem. Miles and miles away, we all know, but do not say, that there are others living under thundering jets, the threat of war. Our jets here are for fun, for demonstration, the "see what we are capable of?" in the resounding drawl of American bravado. Here in California, children point and laugh and smile and try to find the highest of hills to witness the military display.

I do not know these Jews. I know these Jews. I do not know these trees. I know these trees.

The brittle debris of the trees, rust-colored shades of brown, get caught in the fibers of the blanket, and while I hum along to the dulcet familiar melodies of an ancient language, I rub them between my fingers. The leaves turn into a kind of dirt. It, too, is an ancient language: the leaves growing and engaging with the sunlight, and then falling to meet those that went before them, to turn to dust, to again feed the next generation. In all our communities, small rural ones, bustling urban ones, and in far-flung locales, Jews continually reforest themselves where they land.

When the service is over, those who know each other hug, shake hands, pat backs. I help M fold his blanket. It is white and soft, more suited for a pristine linen sofa. Not for the dirt, the ground, and yet, he has shared this white blanket with friends and strangers, so they would be more comfortable. We pull debris from its fibers and brush off the leaves as best we can. M and I laugh about it not being ideal and he says something about comfort not always being comfortable, and I will think about the depths of that comment for months. Our hands meet as we fold the blanket and bring its edges together. It feels like a sacred ritualistic act. I thank him and my daughter, R, and I leave the copse and walk into the sunlight of a limitless California sky.

We then meet up with R's son. To our delight, my daughter and he get on remarkably well and easily. They laugh and share the same frames of references, many around Greek mythology. They ruminate over LEGO creations and create several inside jokes in just a few days. They're connected by more, it seems. Something intangible, invisible. Their antics go on all weekend. My friend and I meet each other's eyes, silently saying *will you look at this? This incredible connection?* These Jewish children will go forward when we are no longer able to, when we spiral down from the tree of life, to meet on the forest floor.

Collective nouns always fascinate me. How a single thing is just the thing, but when there are several, they become something else, something larger, stronger. A group of fighter jets is called a squadron. A group of trees is called a forest. A group of Jews is called a miracle.

Contributors

Melinda Gordon Blum holds an MFA in Creative Nonfiction from UC Riverside-Palm Desert's low-residency program. She is the former managing editor of *The Coachella Review* and a contributor to its book reviews. Her essays have appeared in *The Los Angeles Times, Lunch Ticket, Kveller, The Keepthings, Sun Magazine's* "Readers Write," and other publications. "This Isn't About a Bracelet" is adapted and excerpted from her unpublished memoir *Where Do We Start?: Essays on the Legacies of Survival.* She lives in Los Angeles.

Judy Bolton-Fasman is the author of *ASYLUM: A Memoir of Family Secrets* from Mandel Vilar Press. She has received fellowships, including those from Hedgebrook, the Mineral School, and Virginia Center for Creative Arts for Latino writers. Her essays and reviews have appeared in major newspapers, essay anthologies, and literary magazines. She is a three-time Pushcart Prize nominee, Best of the Net nominee, and a 2024 Best American Essay nominee. She also received a Mass Cultural Grant in 2023. Read more at www.judyboltonfasman.com.

Eileen Vorbach Collins is a Baltimore native. Her work has been widely published, receiving several literary awards, and was twice nominated for a Pushcart Prize. Eileen's essay collection, *Love in the Archives, a Patchwork of True Stories About Suicide Loss,* was a Foreword Indies Finalist and received the Sarton Women's Book Award for Memoir.

Adrienne Dern found new meaning in retirement following a gratifying career in non-profits. She has spent her adult life in the Washington, D.C. area, enjoying all that it has to offer, from the splendor of Great Falls Park to the abundance of art, theater, music and dance. Adrienne welcomed an invitation to join a friend's writing group in 2017 and began to explore her world through personal essays. In September 2019 she self-published a collection of her essays in *Shadows & Reflections: Thoughts on the Light and Dark Stuff of Life*.

Dina Elenbogen is author of the poetry collections *Shore* and *Apples of the Earth*, as well as the memoir *Drawn from Water: an American Poet, an Ethiopian Family, an Israeli Story*. She's received fellowships from the Illinois Arts Council and the Ragdale Foundation. Her work has appeared in anthologies and magazines including *Fury, City of the Big shoulders, Beyond Lament, Lit Hub, Bellevue Literary Review, Brevity, Prairie Schooner, december, Woven Tale Press, Cimmaron Review, Patterson Literary Review, Connecticut River Review, New City Chicago* and other venues. She has an MFA in poetry from the Iowa Writers' Workshop and teaches creative writing at the University of Chicago Writer's Studio. You can find her at www.dinaelenbogen.com

Debbie Feit is an accidental mental health advocate, unrelenting Jewish mother and author of the poetry chapbook *The Power of the Plastic Fork: A Daughter's Highly Unorthodox Kaddish* (Porkbelly Press) in addition to texts to her kids that go unanswered. Her work has appeared in *Kveller, The New York Times, Abandon Journal, HAD, Harbor Review, ONE ART: a journal of poetry*, and on her mother's bulletin board. She is also the author of *The Parent's Guide to Speech and Language Problems* (McGraw-Hill) as well as random rants about her husband's inability to see crumbs on the kitchen counter. Visit her on Instagram @debbiefeit or at debbiefeit.com.

Jennifer Fliss (she/her) is the writer of the story collections *As If She Had a Say* (2023) and *The Predatory Animal Ball* (2021). Her writing has appeared in *F(r)iction, The Rumpus, The Washington Post,* and elsewhere. She can be found via her website www.jenniferflisscreative.com.

Lynne Golodner is the award-winning author of 12 bestselling books including two poetry collections, three novels and seven nonfiction books. A mother of four young adults based in Detroit, Lynne was a journalist in New York and Washington, D.C. and has been the CEO of a marketing company since 2007. Her author brand focuses on creating compelling, strong Jewish characters in emotional stories with universal appeal. She is at work on her fourth novel. Learn more about Lynne at lynnegolodner.com.

Tzivia Gover is a poet and author, whose most recent book, *Dreaming on the Page: Tap into Your Midnight Mind to Supercharge Your Writing*, is an IBPA Gold winner. Her poetry has been published in dozens of journals and anthologies including *The Mom Egg Review, The Other Journal, Pensive*, and *Lilith Magazine*. She has received numerous awards for her writing and a Pushcart Nomination. She shares her poems and poetic translations about the first Hebrew Matriarch, Sarah, in an online publication, *The Life of H: Sarah, Reimagined*. Tzivia teaches, writes, and dreams in western Massachusetts. Learn more at www.thirdhousemoon.com.

Melissa Greenwood has an MFA in creative nonfiction writing from Antioch University Los Angeles. She's been published in *Brevity, The Los Angeles Review*, the *Los Angeles Review of Books, The Manifest-Station, Jewish Literary Journal, Longridge Review*, and elsewhere, including in ELJ's award-winning anthology *Awakenings: Stories of Bodies & Consciousness* and in the journals that have nominated her for literary distinctions: *Meow Meow Pow Pow* (Best Small Fiction), *Kelp Journal* (Best of the Net), and *Gold Man Review* (the Pushcart Prize).

Lisa Grunberger has a doctorate from the University of Chicago Divinity School and has been called a "Jewish Yoga Rabbi." She's a Pushcart nominee, a Temple University Professor, and a first-generation American. *For the Future of Girls* was nominated for an Eric Hoffer Independent Book Award. Her work has appeared in *The New York Times, The Southern Review, Roots Quarterly, The Baffler, The Jewish Literary Journal*. Her play ALMOST

PREGNANT, is published by Next Stage Press. Her memoir-in-progress is *Me and My Makers: A Memoir of Genes, Adoption and Love*. She's a Yoga Therapist and facilitates Mindfulness/Infertility retreats internationally. Schmooze: www.Lisagrunberger.com.

Julia Grunes is a writer from Monroe, NY. She holds a BA in psychology and English (creative writing) from SUNY Geneseo. Her work has previously been published in *Fabula Press*, *Gandy Dancer*, and *Iris Magazine*. Julia spent last year as a Fulbright English Teaching Assistant at IE University in Madrid, Spain. Now, in an effort to support Jewish life, she works as Boston University Hillel's Jewish Life Fellow.

Talya Jankovits is an award-winning writer of poetry, essays, and fiction. Her poetry collection, *girl woman wife mother* (Kelsay Books, 2024), received First Place in Contemporary Poetry in the 2024 Bookfest Awards. She holds her MFA in Creative Writing and resides in Chicago with her husband and four daughters. To read more of her work you can visit her at www.talyajankovits.com.

Gabrielle Ariella Kaplan-Mayer is a spiritual director, author and educator focused on finding holiness in creativity, dreams and intuition. Her personal essays have been featured in *Shondaland*, *NBCThink*, *Lilith*, *WHYY* and many other publications. She's the author of six non-fiction books and several collections of plays for children. Gabrielle is currently working on a memoir about the power of intuition and ongoing conversations with her ancestors. She serves as Ritualwell's Director of Virtual Content and Programs. Reach her at www.gabriellekaplanmayer.com.

Joan Leegant is the author of three award-winning books of fiction. Her latest, *Displaced Persons: Stories*, was a finalist for 2025 National Jewish Book Award, the Association of Jewish Libraries Fiction Award, and a Foreward Indies Award. Formerly a lawyer, for five years Joan was the visiting writer at Bar-Ilan University outside Tel Aviv where she also lectured on American literature and culture under the auspices of the U.S. Embassy and was a volunteer ESL teacher for African refugees and asylum seekers. She lives outside Boston with her family. For more about Joan's work, visit www.joanleegant.com.

Sarah Leibov is a writer, storyteller and advocate helping to save lives by inspiring audiences to pursue genetic screening. Sarah's personal essays have appeared in *HuffPost*, *Newsweek*, *Tablet* and other publications. Her memoir in progress is based on a 2012 article about coping with her younger sister's death from Tay-Sachs disease. "Dancing with My Sister" was published in *Jewish Chicago Magazine* and led to her role speaking about the importance of carrier screening for the Sarnoff Center for Jewish Genetics. Sarah is a Feldenkrais Method creative movement instructor and enjoys sharing her stories onstage and online at sarahleibov.com.

Ellen Levitt is a veteran teacher, writer and photographer. She is the author of the trilogy on The Lost Synagogues of NYC books (www.avotaynu.com) and Walking Manhattan (www.wildernesspress.com). She has written hundreds of articles and essays as well. See her continued documentation of Former Synagogues work on (3) Facebook. She and her husband have two wonderful daughters.

Nina B. Lichtenstein (a.k.a. the Viking Jewess) is a native of Oslo, Norway, who even though she has lived in the U.S. since the mid 1980s, is still a proud Norwegian, and has recently become both a U.S. and Israeli citizen. She has a PhD in French Literature and an MFA in creative nonfiction, is the founder and director of Maine Writers Studio, and the author of *Sephardic Women's Voices: Out of North Africa* (Gaon Books, 2017) and the memoir *Body: My Life in Parts* (Vine Leaves Press, 2025). She is the mother of three grown sons and lives in Maine with her husband.

Matthew Lippman is the author of 8 poetry collections. His latest collection, *We Are All Sleeping With Our Sneakers On (2024)*, is published by Four

Way Books. His previous collection *Mesmerizingly Sadly Beautiful* (2020) is published by Four Way Books. It was the recipient of the 2018 Levis Prize. In 2026 his collection *King of the Jews* will be published by Ben Yehuda Press. In 2027 his collection, *Cry Baby Cry*, will be published by Four Way Books.

Ana Miriam Lublin is a small business owner, performer, author, and songwriter. Her essay, "Are Those Real" was published in the LGBTQ anthology *One Teacher in Ten*. Creating groups that facilitate creating community brings her great joy. She runs several writing groups and a book club. Her novel-in-progress focuses on the dramatic survival of her grandparents and father during the Holocaust and their lives before and after the war. She also plans to tell these stories as a performer. The fragility of her family's survival leaves her incredibly grateful to be alive.

Aliza Marton is a Los Angeles-based Judaica and nature artist known for her mastery of oil on canvas and her signature technique—blending abstract fluid acrylic with realism on wood panels, finished with resin. Her work reflects a deep spiritual connection, often weaving biblical passages into scenes of nature and Jewish life. Beyond creating, Aliza has guided hundreds of students in the Jewish community through art instruction. However, her greatest fulfillment comes from seeing collectors form a personal bond with her work, making it a meaningful part of their homes. Her artwork is now cherished in private collections worldwide.

Sandell Morse—sandellmorse.com—is the author of the memoir, *The Spiral Shell, A French Village Reveals Its Secrets of World War II*. Morse's essays have been noted in the *Best American Essays* series, published in Creative Nonfiction, Ploughshares, and the New England Review, among others. She has won the Michael Steinberg essay prize, been nominated for Best of the net, and two Pushcart prizes. Morse has been a Tennessee Williams Scholar at the Sewanee Writers' Conference, an Associate Artist at the Atlantic Center for the Creative Arts, a resident at Hewnoaks, Marble House Project, and the Virginia Center for the Creative Arts.

Robbi Nester is a retired college educator and author of five books of poetry, the latest forthcoming from Shanti Arts sometime this year. She has also edited three anthologies. Currently, she curates and hosts two monthly virtual poetry series. Learn more at her website, http://www.robbinester.net.

Rochelle Newman-Carrasco credits her love of culture, comedy, and community to her Lower East Side NYC roots. The co-author of *ZigZag*, a bilingual English-Spanish children's book, her essays have appeared in *The New York Times*, *Lilith*, *The Forward*, *The Ethel*, *Off Assignment*, *The Independent* and more. She holds a BFA, Theater from UC Irvine and an MFA, Writing from Antioch University, Los Angeles. She is currently querying a memoir based on her solo theater show *Hip Bones and Cool Whip*. A pioneering voice in the field of inclusive marketing and advertising, she is known for leveraging strategy and storytelling.

Ronit Plank is a writer, teacher, and editor whose work has appeared in *The Atlantic*, *Poets & Writers*, *The Rumpus*, *Lilith*, *The NYT,* and elsewhere. Her memoir WHEN SHE COMES BACK about the loss of her mother to the guru Bhagwan Shree Rajneesh and their eventual reconciliation was a Book Riot Best True Crime Book and finalist for the Housatonic Award and National Indie Excellence Award. Her story collection HOME IS A MADE-UP PLACE won both the Eludia and Page Turner Awards for fiction. She is creative nonfiction editor at *The Citron Review* and hosts the podcast Let's Talk Memoir.

Amy Rogers is a journalist who spent 15 years writing about food and culture for NPR station WFAE (Charlotte, NC) and many other publications. Her books include *Hungry for Home: Stories of Food from Across the Carolinas*. As an editor and workshop presenter, she has helped hundreds of people hone their skills and find satisfaction in their writing. Rogers is currently at work on a reported memoir about people facing and solving problems of hunger and housing injustice. Visit her at amyrogers.net.

Seth Schindler is an anthropologist, sculptor and writer of fiction and nonfiction. He has worked as Curator at the Arizona State Museum and served as NEH Fellow at the University of Arizona and Weatherhead Resident Scholar at the School for Advanced Research. His short stories have appeared in many literary magazines and have been finalists for the Gival Press Short Story Award and the Tucson Book Festival Literary Awards. His novelette *The Time Golem* was recently published by ELJ Editions. The University of Arizona Press published his book about the plight of the food insecure in America today, *Sowing the Seeds of Change*.

Jena Schwartz is a Jewish mother who wants to make sure you've eaten lately. Her work has appeared in *Tikkun*, *Emerge Literary Journal*, the *Times of Israel* and *On Being* blogs, *Cognoscenti*, *Jewish Writing Project*, *Siddur Lev Shalem*, and the anthologies *Calling Out: Psalms for Today* and *On Being 40(ish)*, among other publications. Author of *Fierce Encouragement: 201 Writing Prompts for Staying Grounded in Fragile Times* and three previous books, Jena is a Certified Jewish Studio Project Creative Facilitator and Poet-in-Residence at the Jewish Community of Amherst. Subscribe to *Dispatches from Daily Life* at jenaschwartz.substack.com and visit her at www.jenaschwartz.com.

Amy Shimshon-Santo was born on Tovaangar land in current day LA and has immediate family in the Southwest, the Middle East, and South America. Her most recent books are *Random Experiments in Bioluminescence* (eco-feminist, plurilingual poems), and *Piecework: Ethnographies of Place* (essays on arts education, migration, and community). She is the author of three poetry collections, a limited edition chapbook, and numerous academic essays for *GeoHumanities*, *Urban Education* and more. Amy has edited anthologies and special editions for the Braille Institute Library, the LA Public Library, Revista de Crítica Cultura, Libretto Magazine, Illinois Open Publishing Network, and UC Press.

Megan Vered's essays and interviews have appeared in HuffPost, Kveller, Shondaland, The Linden Review, High Country News, The Rumpus, the

Los Angeles Review of Books, and the Writer's Chronicle, among others. She was long listed for the Disquiet 2022 Literary Prize and a finalist for the Bellingham Review's 2021 Annie Dillard Award for Creative Nonfiction. Megan holds an MFA in Creative Writing from Vermont College of Fine Arts, is on the board of Heyday Books and facilitates local and international writing workshops. Her memoir is currently under review for publication.

Mimi Zieman is a physician and the author of *Tap Dancing on Everest*, a memoir about the risks we take to become our truest selves. The book was named Best Memoir of 2024 by the American Writing Awards among other first-place honors. Her play *The Post-Roe Monologues* has been performed in multiple cities and essays have appeared in USA Today, *Newsweek,* Salon, *The Sun Magazine, Ms. Magazine, The Forward,* and elsewhere. Her Substack newsletter, *Medicine, Mountains & More* combines medical news with inspiration from art and nature. Learn more at www.mimiziemanmd.com.

Julie Zuckerman is the author of *The Book of Jeremiah: A Novel in Stories* (Press 53, 2019). Her fiction and non-fiction have appeared in *CRAFT, Atlas & Alice, Jewish Fiction, Salt Hill,* and *Sixfold,* among others. She hosts the monthly Literary Modiin author series. She is currently preparing a sequel novel-in-stories for submission and is at work on a new novel. A native of Connecticut, she now lives in Israel with her husband and four children. Subscribe to Julie's monthly author newsletter for book recommendations, literary events, resources for writers, recipes and more.

Editors

Diane Gottlieb, MSW, MEd, MFA, is the editor of the award-winning anthology *Awakenings: Stories of Body & Consciousness* (ELJ Editions) and of the micro-chapbook volume *Grieving Hope* (ELJ Editions). Her writing appears in *Brevity, River Teeth, Witness, Adroit Journal, Colorado Review, Florida Review, SmokeLong Quarterly, 2023 Best Microfiction, The Rumpus, Hippocampus Magazine,* and many other lovely places. Diane is the winner of *Tiferet Journal*'s 2021 Writing Contest in nonfiction, longlisted in 2023 and 2024 at *Wigleaf*'s Top 50, and a finalist for *Hole in the Head Review*'s 2024 Charles Simic Poetry Prize and *The Florida Review*'s 2023 Editor's Prize for Creative Nonfiction. She is the Special Projects Editor at ELJ Editions and the Prose/CNF Editor for *Emerge Literary Journal*. You can find her at dianegottlieb.com and @DianeGotAuthor.

Erika Dreifus is the author of *Birthright: Poems* and *Quiet Americans: Stories*, which was named an American Library Association/Sophie Brody Medal Honor Title for outstanding achievement in Jewish literature. An active literary consultant and advocate, Erika teaches at Baruch College/CUNY; serves on the boards of The Artists Against Antisemitism and the Leo Baeck Institute; and is a Sami Rohr Jewish Literary Institute fellow. She lives in New York City. Web: ErikaDreifus.com.

www.ingramcontent.com/pod-product-compliance
Lightning Source LLC
Chambersburg PA
CBHW031321160426
43196CB00007B/607